A LIFE'S WORK

—

FATHERS AND SONS

BEN BRADLEE

AND

QUINN BRADLEE

WITH OBSERVATIONS BY

SALLY QUINN

SIMON & SCHUSTER
NEW YORK   LONDON   TORONTO   SYDNEY

Simon & Schuster
1230 Avenue of the Americas
New York, NY 10020

First Simon & Schuster hardcover edition May 2010

SIMON & SCHUSTER and colophon are registered trademarks of Simon & Schuster, Inc.

For information about special discounts for bulk purchases, please contact Simon & Schuster Special Sales at 1-866-506-1949 or business@simonandschuster.com.

The Simon & Schuster Speakers Bureau can bring authors to your live event. For more information or to book an event, contact the Simon & Schuster Speakers Bureau at 1-866-248-3049 or visit our website at www.simonspeakers.com.

Designed by Nancy Singer

Manufactured in the United States of America

10 9 8 7 6 5 4 3 2 1

Library of Congress Cataloging-in-Publication Data
Bradlee, Benjamin C.
A life's work : fathers and sons / Ben Bradlee and Quinn Bradlee ; with observations by Sally Quinn.
    p. cm.
1. Bradlee, Benjamin C. 2. Bradlee, Quinn 3. Journalists—United States—Biography.
4. Fathers and sons—United States. I. Bradlee, Quinn. II. Quinn, Sally. III. Title.
  PN4874.B6615A3 2010
  070.92'2—dc22
  [B]
                                                            2010005909

ISBN 978-0-684-80895-6

FOR SALLY

FOR PARY

FOR BENNY, DINO, AND MARINA,
ALL OF WHOM WE LOVE AND WHO MEAN
SO MUCH TO US IN OUR LIVES

PROLOGUE

This book is about fathers and sons and how they forge relationships. It isn't just about the two of us. It is about all fathers and sons. It isn't just about a particular time in our lives. It's about a whole life span—a father watching his son grow, learn, and flourish, a son reaping the benefit of his father's experience, wisdom, and values. It's about a special bond between two guys. For us it was in the woods, both with each of our fathers. There are two things that matter—time spent together and love. You cannot have a real father-son relationship without being together. Nor can you have one without love. Sometimes it takes work. Not just during the early years, or the teenage years, or the midlife years. It takes a lifetime. That's why we decided to call this book, *A Life's Work.*

Ben and Quinn Bradlee

CONTENTS

Contents

PART THREE

CONTENTS

A LIFE'S WORK

PART ONE

———

Quinn I thought my dad was God. He was like an emperor. He was like a king. I thought he knew everything in the world and he was my teacher. I learned all my life lessons being in the woods with my father. I learned more there than in school, by far. My dad knows all the names of the trees and the plants and the flowers. He knows everything about the woods and it is amazing.

Ben's father, Frederick Josiah Bradlee, Jr.

FATHERS

Ben   I thought my father was the cat's meow. Not because he was a college football star or a successful banker. No, by the time I became alert, he'd lost his job during the Depression, never to have another great one. But he worked hard, persevered, and came out of the Depression with his shoulders straight and squared.

My father, Frederick Josiah Bradlee, Jr., or "Beebo" or just "B," was a Walter Camp All-American football player at Harvard. He never became a public figure after football but he made his way in banking, eventually becoming vice president of Bank America Blair Company, a small branch bank in Massachusetts. It's not that he brought any original concepts to banking. He didn't. He was a banker because people trusted him. B Bradlee was dead honest, and looked it.

In addition to his athleticism, he was known as one of the world's most honest people. The city of Boston was filled with corruption when Mayor James Michael Curley was in office.

When an independent commission was set up to investigate the mayor and his cronies, my father, who had no distinction except his reputation for honesty and his past athleticism, was named chairman of it.

We—my father; my mother, Josephine; my older brother, Freddy; my younger sister, Connie; and I—lived at 267 Beacon Street in Boston's Back Bay, a hundred yards down the street from the house where my father was born at 211 Beacon and not far from the apartment at 295 Beacon that he and my mother lived in when they were first married. Our Beacon Street residence, his third but not my parents' last, had a direct view of the houses that had a direct view of the Charles River.

Dad's parents lived a few blocks away in the brownstone my father grew up in. Dad's dad, the original Frederick Josiah Bradlee, was a relentlessly ordinary man. He managed a branch of a bank on Arlington Street in Boston. He had a white mustache and an even whiter head of short-cropped hair. I can't remember him ever saying or doing anything that had any distinction to it. Grandma Bessie wasn't particularly attractive herself, but she played the piano beautifully and was a student of Artur Schnabel, one of the great pianists. At the age of seventy she'd go down to New York City for lessons, which was a big deal. Maybe she had something going with him, but she was not sexy, to say the least. Backed by the weight of her stout fingers, her rings would clank as she put them on the piano top and started playing.

Like his dad, my dad was very quiet. My mother talked a lot, but my father was quite silent. She laughed often, while he preferred to smile, and always before he laughed. You could see a smile forming in my father's face, whereas my mother bared her great white teeth immediately (which we teased her about endlessly). Even after the Crash, when he was going through a rough patch, I didn't feel bad for my dad. He wouldn't let you feel bad for him. He had great joie de vivre and it spilled over into our house.

When my father came home at night, we'd all go upstairs to the second-floor living room, where my parents would have a cocktail while we listened to the news and then *Amos 'n Andy* on the Atwater-Kent radio. My dad would read two evening papers, handing the sports section off to me when he was through with it so I could calculate the baseball players' batting averages. Then we'd go down to the dining room and eat supper; we were through at a quarter of eight. There wasn't a whole lot of family conversation and we weren't a terribly intellectual family, to say the least, but our house was always filled with laughter and teasing.

Unlike most of their friends in those days, B and Jo spent a lot of time with their children. Still, we had nannies who helped take care of my brother, my sister, and me. There was one in particular—a Swiss girl named Sally who was fantastic. She lived on the third floor with just us kids. She'd run around the entire floor with no clothes on. At eighteen, she had a beautiful body, boobs, the whole package. I knew the female form very well by the age of ten.

Beebo had three thirty-yard-line tickets to Harvard's home football games. He, my mother, and I would sit with his teammates, three of them all-Americans themselves: Stan Pennuck, Eddie Mahan, and famed Crimson captain Charlie Brickley, who right around that time went to jail for running a bucket shop. Big men that they were, they were quite obvious and people in the stadium would point at them like they were celebrities. I felt my father was well known, but he wasn't.

———

When the Great Depression arrived on Beacon Street, we went from a maid, a cook, and nurses to making our own beds, cleaning our own rooms, and cooking our own meals. Then my father lost his fifty-thousand-dollar-a-year job and with it a bit of the male dignity that comes from providing for the family. I remember feeling sad that he'd lost his job, though I didn't really understand how important it was for a man to have a job.

My mother always had more money than my father and when B lost his job, my parents depended on the charity of her father to pay the bills. My grandfather was a Wall Street lawyer, but not a very interesting one. Carl de Gersdorff was a partner in Cravath, de Gersdorff, Swaine & Wood, a prestigious and pioneering law firm that represented the railroad companies as they pushed west and later worked with Henry Luce and Time/Life. It was a considerable firm, in which my grandfather appeared to play no role at all. He specialized in tax law and worked with widows. They dropped the "De Gersdorff" when he left the firm.

My father didn't get along with his father-in-law, who was barely tolerant of him or anyone else, really. De Gersdorff sat at the head of the table, though you'd think it was the center of the universe, where his butler, a Swede named Eckman, fussed around him. Eckman's only real job was to take care of my grandfather—which for the most part involved keeping his glass of scotch full—and the rest of us were lucky to get served. My grandfather was nice to my mother in his own way, mostly by writing checks. But we were all made aware of the fact that he was the benefactor. Needy or not, I never got the sense my grandfather was glad to see my father. And I definitely got the sense that my father wasn't glad to see him. Grandparents, in other words, were not a big deal for me.

As much as I dreaded our holiday visits to New York City to see my grandparents, I was able to find sanctuary in my grandfather's library. I didn't read a lot as a kid but at one point his books caught my eye. He owned a couple of originals bound by a famous bookbinder in London named Joseph Zaehnsdorf. The first page of those books had a fancy design that he created, sometimes marbleized paper, and his name was on the very top of the back of the second page. My father shared my interest in bookbinding, so we'd escape from my tyrannical grandfather by taking refuge in his library.

———

After the Depression my father couldn't find a regular job and, for the first time I could remember, he started coming home before five in the afternoon. I think he felt despair. Everything he'd done before then had been a great success and then he was nothing. But he wasn't visibly upset. In fact he was marvelous about his misfortune. I learned a lot from watching him during that time and came to quickly understand that there were going to be ups and downs in life.

He soon took on various odd jobs. At one point he ran the maintenance crew of the Museum of Fine Arts in Boston; he kept the books of a Canadian molybdenum mine for some dough; he was a trustee and the treasurer of the Essex County Club, which meant our membership was free; he balanced the books for the Dexter School and then St. Mark's School in exchange for Freddy's and my tuition. He spent a few months selling a commercial deodorant, which some of his college buddies had invested in, to big Boston companies whose officers he knew. In an effort to demonstrate the power of Sanovan, he even scrubbed a railroad car for the Boston & Maine Railroad in front of an audience of higher-ups there. I can remember him sort of being down that day. None of his friends did that kind of work. But he did it, and he did it with a good spirit.

For years our family vehicle was a four-door Chevy painted a god-awful sky blue that the car dealer had promised would attract maximum attention. We children, especially Freddy, were embarrassed when B put a Sanovan tire cover on the spare tire over the rear bumper. My father was just proud of the deal he got on the car.

There was no lack of work in my family. When I was about twelve, my mother went to work as a salesperson for her friends Adelaide Sohier and Emma Lawrence, proprietors of ADEM dress shop on Newbury Street in Boston. With a loan from her father, she eventually bought the shop and ran it herself. Solo business trips to buy clothes from wholesalers in New York allowed her some independence. Back in Boston, B was working hard even when he didn't have a real job.

Even in the Depression, work wasn't just about money. You had to continue to pay back the good fortune you inherited, even when it was nowhere to be seen. My mother, who was so uncomfortable with anything that wasn't letter perfect, worked with inner-city kids in Boston. Later, during World War II, she helped care for French children sent to America to escape the war, which eventually led to her being awarded the Legion of Honor, the highest civilian award given by the French government. Equally amazing, my father kept the books for churches even though you could never get him into one.

The Depression turned out to be a great thing for my family. It brought us even closer together.

BEVERLY

Ben   In the bowels of the Depression, my family was given an estate on the North Shore of Massachusetts, in Beverly, where the beach first takes over the coastline. The Putnams, vague relatives of ours on my father's side, loaned it to us to live in, provided we took care of the twenty acres of wooded land, the barns, and the house. There'd be a Beverly in my life from then on.

The house was an old Victorian place that sat atop a hill overlooking the ocean a mile to the east, the town of Beverly to the west and Salem Harbor in the distance to the south. My mother had a lot of taste but not a lot of dough, so for the most part, the house stayed as we found it and wasn't very fancy. The piano that my mother played (and insisted we play) was kept in the living room. Every room in the house had a fireplace and there was wood in every one of them. The house once belonged to a ship owner who'd wallpapered all three stories' worth of walls, including in the living room, which was covered with the most beautiful antique, hand-painted, Chinese wallpaper of blue birds flying among flowers, without a single bird or flower repeated all the way through. Connie, Freddy, and I played "murder" and all sorts of other games in the twenty-odd rooms up on the hill. It was a comfortable place but the lack of heat and running water meant that every autumn I helped my dad close down the house for the winter and we moved into the late-seventeenth-century cottage on the main road that zigzagged up the coast to Gloucester.

The Beverly place was informally called "Witchwood" on account of local legend that said it was connected to the Salem witch trials. The story goes that the people who were charged with being witches used to collect there either to do their witchcraft or to run away from the crazies who thought they were witches. Someone in my family painted WITCHWOOD on the wood-paneled side door of a secondhand station wagon we had there.

Beverly was my and, as far as I know, my dad's first exposure to the outdoors. But somehow he knew everything about trees and birds. He was a student of birds and bird calls, educated by a record of robin and chickadee recordings that we'd listen to on a cheap little stand-up record player in the study.

I knew every inch of that place. I climbed every tree and rock, slogged through the swamp collecting snakes, bugs, and butterflies, and dawdled around a tiny pond that didn't amount to anything except a place to breed mosquitoes. The first year we were there I built a tree house in a spruce tree. I should've chosen an oak with big branches and lots of space instead of the spruce with all its branches in every which direction. Finally I cleared a spot and put up the plywood walls. I spent a lot of time building it, maintaining it, cutting a window on one side; after that I didn't know what to do up there.

But we had work to do to hold up our end of the bargain with the Putnams.

THE WOODS

Ben Pop and I worked out in the woods from the beginning. Since it was messy and all but abandoned, we tackled the driveway first. It turned off Route 127/Hale Street and wheeled through the woods, turning in on itself the whole way up. We raked the stones, took down trees, dug up roots when they started to cross the driveway, and even planted flowers alongside the way. From the get-go, my father loved the woods. He loved working out there with me, but he loved working out there, period.

B had never worked in the woods before. True to the terms of our unwritten contract with the Putnams, he just went out and started chopping down dead trees, clearing brush, and cleaning the place up. Then I did, too. I don't even remember ever asking him; I just did it because that's what my dad did. It wasn't a chore and I didn't get paid for it. People always wanted to be around my father and working in the woods at Beverly gave me a chance to spend some time with him.

It would seem that a saw is a saw is a saw. But we found out quickly that there's more to it. We never had a resident expert but my dad had a friend named George von Lengerke Meyer, Jr., or "Bey," who knew how to use an ax and a two-man saw. When he and my dad worked in the woods together, they sweated and they swore but they didn't talk a hell of a lot. It was on-the-job training with my dad and old man Meyer, who was always nice to me. A two-man saw is at least six feet of wobbly, flexible steel that can be bent all the way around so the handles are together. Bypassing the difficult first cut with any saw, we'd chop a V in the trunk with an ax. The V pointed to where we wanted the tree to fall. Then we'd start sawing, my dad on one end, me on the other. Cutting with a saw is a pulling action more than a pushing one. And a two-man saw is all about pulling while the other guy takes a moment's rest. I'd pull it back, then he'd pull it back. I'd pull it back, then he'd pull it back. Now, B was about five foot ten, broad-shouldered, and strong as an ox, weighing in at 185 pounds from the time he was a football fullback until the end of his life. At ten, I was a foot shorter and another foot narrower. I'm sure my dad was pushing the saw while I pulled back.

If we didn't keep cutting through the slot that we made, if we pulled up on the saw or it wasn't pulled absolutely level, it would bind. Breaking the saw free from the jaws of the trunk was tough and it'd be four times as hard to cut through the trunk as a result.

Not to mention that jamming the saw drove the guy who kept the blade straight crazy; for years that was me.

We'd position the cut so it would get deeper and deeper until the tree would finally fall under its own weight. If we wanted it to fall to the right, we'd cut a gap in the right and start sawing on the left. Sometimes, we'd jam iron wedges into the cut as the saw got in and then wedge the tree. The good guys could place it on a dime.

Blight was wiping out beech trees in New England at the time and provided more than enough work for the first few years. Half the woods at Beverly were dead beech trees. Extremely hard and two to three feet wide, they could take an hour to cut down, that is, if you could keep the saw going. In reality, it took my dad and me a couple of hours of damned hard work. By the time we sawed through it, got it to fall where we wanted it to, and then started taking the limbs off, the day would be over. But my dad never did things half-assed. You always finish a job.

We'd cut the limbs off without protocol, split the trunk into firewood with a steel wedge and sledgehammer, and pile the brush to burn. My dad taught me how to prepare the ground for burning so the fire wouldn't run across the woods.

The burning of the brush was a ceremonial task with my family. Even my mother took part by picking up twigs with her thumb and forefinger as if they were some stranger's dirty underwear and putting them on the fire. Her side of the family would turn up their noses at that but she did it, even though she didn't like it very much.

Besides my mother's occasional involvement, the woods were my dad's and my domain. My brother, Freddy, was bored out of his mind out there. He'd rather be practicing a monologue, trying out his accents, or perfecting his talent for mimicry, a skill he shared with my father. He was on his way to a career in the theater, not in the woods.

Freddy didn't miss any riveting conversations. My dad and I didn't talk a hell of a lot when we worked out there; we didn't wrestle with great issues. We just did the work. If there was some big family problem I guess it would come up, but life wasn't like that.

Whoever got up first in the morning would make breakfast. By ten-thirty, Pop and I would be at the barn up on the hill picking up the axes and saws, then be on our way to the week's project. We worked less in the summer than in the fall or spring, but we worked a lot in the winter. Regardless of the season, my dad was in his wool shirt and khakis every weekend, holding up our end of the bargain. Soon there were no dead trees, no dead branches, no dead stumps, and no messy undergrowth. We ended up with twenty acres that were beautiful, without being soigné. It didn't look like an arboretum, just pristine woods.

For a novice of the woods, B was incredibly comfortable there. More than just surviving, he was adapting. My father never had a great job after the Depression, but he was respected by his friends, some of them senators and congressmen, and admired by his family for putting his nose down and his ass up. No work was too menial.

That was a lesson my father's brothers, Sargent and Malcolm, never seemed to learn, though. My lazy uncles would come over on the weekends, sometimes with my dad's other buddies, and load up on martinis for lunch. Full of liquor and not having done any physical labor since they were kids, they'd go out in the woods and cut down trees, sweating pure gin. Thank God they didn't have chain saws.

I'd sometimes get stuck on the opposite end of the two-man saw with one of my unskilled, out-of-shape uncles on the other end. My uncles were kind of lumpen and they weren't very good at anything, but I was never as strong as they or my father. I couldn't lift quite as much or work quite as long. But I was as physically coordinated and with a lot of effort I could do everything they did, which made me feel like one of the boys. I was proud to be able to work with those old goats.

POLIO

Ben I missed one summer in the woods. One Sunday in May 1935, Freddy Hubbell, an eighth-grade classmate at St. Mark's School, and I spent all afternoon sprinting, running, jumping, and throwing the hammer and discus at the track. After we showered, dressed, and ate, we sat on our beds, each of us in immense pain. A few hours later we were both lying in the infirmary with flu-like fevers and aches. By noon Monday we were sharing an ambulance to Boston, thirty miles away.

When I arrived at our Beacon Street house, my father and the family doctor, George Denny, were waiting for me outside. Dad, calm and steady, carried me in his arms up two flights of stairs to my sister's room. I didn't know it at the time, but my family didn't have the money to send me to Massachusetts General Hospital, where Freddy Hubell went. He died there two days later from polio.

For the first two weeks, polio feels like the flu—aches, pains, fever—and the damage that it is going to do gets done. And then all of a sudden, the aches and pains disappear. The fever is gone and you're left with the condition that you're in. I was sick as a dog those first few weeks but I remember either my mother or father being there in the room at all times.

When the doctor came to assess the damage, my father and mother stood next to the bed. They never talked about, or even showed, their fears despite the doctor's frowns. Raise your eyebrow, now the other, frown, shut your left eye, your right, wink, sniff, move your lips and tongue, swallow, take a deep breath, cough, wiggle your fingers, move your elbows, lift your shoulders. That's where polio got me. I couldn't raise my shoulders more than a few inches off the bed. My gut muscles weren't working, not to mention my legs. I felt fine but I couldn't move.

But I could cry, and so could my parents. They were strong, though, especially my father, and before long we tackled the reality of my paralysis. I'd have to wear braces fitted with wooden footboards to ensure that the weight of the sheets didn't bend my feet down and level them, a possibility that everyone was making a big fuss about. And someone would have to carry me to the tub twice a day and to the toilet, as needed. During his breakfast time, my dad lifted me out of bed, down the hall and into the hot bath, then back to my bed. He'd do it again at night. I don't think there is a thirteen-year-old child that I ever could have lifted out of bed into a tub, twice a day. My all-American dad carried me with ease. When I think of my dad today, I think of that strength and that support.

As soon as I was ready to move, I was back in an ambulance (paid for by friends of my parents) and on my way to the country. My dad carried me right up to bed again. I was in there for the summer—June, July, and August. From my bedroom window, I could see the tree house I'd built. The beech tree blight continued and my dad worked in the woods every weekend, sometimes alone, sometimes with his buddies, for five, six, seven hours a day. I couldn't go out. I couldn't see him. I couldn't hear him.

At night, my father and I listened to Red Sox games on the radio. During the day he was out in the woods and I was in bed. Freddy would be rattling around the house talking to himself, perfecting his lines. Connie was getting ready to start collecting boyfriends. I spent the time studying horse racing. My father advanced me two hundred fictitious dollars to bet on the horses at Suffolk Downs. I studied the entries and their past performances, recorded my bets and my dad and I listened to the results on the radio. By Labor Day, I'd made a twenty-five-dollar profit, which my father paid me.

My father installed a pair of trapeze bars over my bed so I could pull myself up and move from one side of the bed to the other, which had the added benefit of my developing a fairly strong chest. My dad and I talked about me walking again but it was Leo Cronan, a Notre Dame athlete who spent his summers back east teaching youngsters like me how to catch, throw, and tackle, who got me seriously thinking about walking again.

Leo would come by every night to eat leftover cookies and milk (a Depression dinner) and check in on me. At some point, he'd decided to dedicate the summer of 1935 to me and my legs. My parents knew nothing of our project until one night at the end of June, when, after a couple of sessions of Leo supporting me under my shoulders as I gradually put more and more weight on my feet and catching me when I fell, he called them up to my bedroom. There I was, the pain of the braces digging into my crotch damn near splitting me in two, but standing.

Over the next few months, I progressed so that I could stand without the braces, though my dad still had to lift me downstairs and into bed. Soon I could walk. Not well—I'd fall down quite a lot—but I could walk. It was plainly going to get better.

Years later I wrote about how I knew I would walk again the entire time I was sick. My editor kept crossing out "knew" in my draft and suggesting I was "persuaded" or "really, really thought" I would be okay. But I knew. I'm a blind optimist so I don't think of things that will never happen. We never get all the bad things. I think we find a way around them and tolerate them.

By the time school started in the fall, I could walk without limping but my belly muscles had been paralyzed so I had to wear a corset to keep my stomach from sagging. I was "recovered" and planned my return to sports. I played baseball later that year, even football in my senior year, but I never could run after I had polio. The baseball team's three polio survivors—second baseman Bob Potter, whose father had been on the Harvard baseball team; Bill Parsons, the catcher who became a minister; and I—would race around the bases. Parsons was even slower than I was, but everybody would laugh to see us chugging away to come in last in a dead heat.

I'd gone from a standard little kid—I could skip, I could sprint, I was agile and athletic—to a high schooler who could barely beat his mother to the goal line and back. There I was, the son of an all-American football player, and I couldn't run.

But it didn't matter. My father didn't put any kind of pressure on me to play football, or any sports for that matter. In the first place, I was much smaller than he was, and considering that I couldn't run after I had polio, I think he was very proud that I even made the damned team.

SONS

Ben My dad and I always shared an interest in sports. We didn't participate together much, except for playing golf and a little tennis. My family belonged to two country clubs, to which we got memberships for free because my father kept the books. One was a little country club that had four tennis courts, including three grass courts, and the other was the Essex County Club, which had a golf course and lots of grass and clay tennis courts. Before I got polio I was a junior mixed doubles champion of Massachusetts.

B wasn't a great tennis player—his knees weren't any good— but he was a canny player. After polio, tennis became impossible for me. I couldn't run and I was just hopeless. So the emphasis shifted to golf, which was really too subtle a game for my dad. He loved to whack the ball as hard as he could but he had no idea where it was going. I think he did it to please my mother, who for her part would hit the ball a hundred times and it'd never go in the air. I was their caddy.

My brother never harbored any hopes of being a star athlete. He played a little tennis, but it was a joke. He had no interest in sports or the woods, preferring the stage to the stadium. Tolerated but far from accepted, Freddy was very much a loner and had a tough time at St. Mark's (he was "asked to leave"), then at Brooks School (he was kicked out for smoking two days before he was due to graduate), then at Harvard (he left after only a few months without telling anyone he was bound for New York). We grew apart as teenagers—he was an outsider, I was an insider, at least for a little while—and I didn't understand him. Nor did I care to then.

My father, on the other hand, embraced the difficulties that Freddy felt. He knew his oldest son was gay before the rest of us did. You'd have thought he'd be totally floored and unable to cope but he was the one who handled it best. The football jock understood it, whereas my mother, the sophisticated and "cultured" one, just smiled.

It still surprises me how fantastic my father was with Freddy. They never spent much time together. They didn't have the physical closeness that my dad and I had from all the time we spent working in the woods together or playing sports. But when it was a question of support, there was no difference between Freddy and me. My dad was equally supportive of us both. I admired him for that and it always impressed me. I think watching my dad with my brother made me realize that fathers and sons don't have to have everything in common. In fact, they seldom do.

————

As much as polio changed life at school, it didn't impact life in the woods. I was back out there working with my dad the following summer. My return to the woods was no great event. Having fully recovered from polio and having never been the world's most self-aware person, I didn't feel any different, except that my chest muscles were stronger from pulling myself around on the trapeze bar. However, the saw wasn't pulling with any more ease. Maybe B just started to take a long-deserved rest on the other end.

Polio was *the* big incident in my youth and my father was a big physical presence during that time. He was always there for me when I was sick, which tightened our relationship. But his support wasn't limited to my time with polio. If I got in trouble (and I did), I went to my dad. When I was sixteen, I smashed up the family car. I was driving in Beverly and tried to pass a car, but there wasn't room. I got smacked, veered off the road, and hit a tree. More scared than hurt, I walked home and left the car in the ditch, which made no sense at all. My dad arrived soon after I did and after seeing that I was all right, took charge of handling the accident, the car, the this, the that. He always fixed things, which is why I always went to him.

My father wasn't just there for me and his family, he was usefully solicitous of others. He was no big shot and he didn't have the means to be excessively charitable, but people came to him for help and advice. Straight and completely honest, people wanted to be around my dad. Our house was always open and there were always friends there.

We lived for free and worked in Beverly, winter weekends in the cottage, summers in the big house up the hill, from 1932 until one afternoon in the summer of 1945. The estate had always been for sale, advertised by a sign in front of the cottage on the main road. The driveway was terribly complicated and once you made your way up to the house, if you weren't going to stop you went around a circle and then rejoined the driveway and went out. One afternoon B and Jo were sitting on the porch having cocktails, when an unknown car pulled up and drove around the circle twice.

"What in God's name does he want?" my mother asked.

"I don't know," my father said. "He's probably looking to buy the place, since it's for sale."

Now for the first time in years, my mother went into a sweat.

She loved the place and wasn't about to lose it. An elderly relative long forgotten in some convent had recently passed away and left my mother ten thousand dollars. She announced that she was going to call the owner and offer him half her inheritance for the whole place.

"You can't do that," my father said. "Two houses, three barns and twenty acres of beautiful woods for five thousand dollars? You can't offer him that."

But she did. They wouldn't take it, but by God they would take ten thousand dollars, and suddenly this gorgeous place was ours.

My dad used to dress like a total slob there. His square face rested below a bald pate, the remaining wispy, curly blond hairs always filled with tiny burns from brush or something that had singed him. One day a different car drove up and came around the circle. The driver got out and asked whether the owner was around, thinking my father couldn't be the head of the estate, given that he was so badly dressed. My father smiled and allowed as how he was the owner.

————

I graduated from high school in 1939 and went to Harvard, as generations of Bradlee boys before me had done. Right about then, girls reared their marvelous heads and I began to spend less time in the woods with my dad. We always had a ceremonial couple of hours out there each weekend but it wasn't like the time I'd spent as a kid.

I was commissioned into the navy two hours after I graduated from college (I had joined the naval ROTC) and a few hours before I got married. On the way to the church, my old man asked me if there was anything I wanted to know about sex. Twenty years old and having never slept with another girl besides my wife-to-be, I didn't know anything about sex. My father and I never talked about girls. There was a whole lot I needed and wanted to know about sex but I was as embarrassed as he was so I told him I thought I was okay in that department.

A month later, I left New York on the U.S.S. *Philip,* a destroyer, off for war in the Pacific. My father had served in the army, though he never went overseas. He was very proud of me and very involved in my navy career. At sea, I couldn't write home saying that I was on the shores off Guadalcanal. But my father knew a senior naval officer in New England, who would keep him informed about the whereabouts of the *Philip.* He knew what campaigns, what fleet, what task force the *Philip* was in, so my dad knew quite a lot about where the hell I was. When I returned to Beverly on home leave, my father knew all about our landings in the Solomons and Marianas, all about the nightly raids we took up the Strait of Bougainville. Sitting in front of the fireplace, he asked me everything about where I'd been, what I'd seen, and where we were going next.

I sailed 295,000 miles in my navy career, sometimes spending as much as sixty days at sea at a time. I missed lots of things more than working in the woods. After the war, I'd go up to Beverly maybe once a summer to see my parents. B continued to work in the woods there alone or with his friends, until his knees began to hurt. Years later, the house burned down and my parents eventually moved into the cottage on the main road and lived there off and on for the rest of their lives. For the first time since college, at the very end of his life, he put on a little weight.

I admired my father enormously, except when he drank too much in his later years. My siblings and I dreaded when my parents entertained, because my dad would disappear in the middle of the cocktail hour, pretending he needed a new bottle of this or that. Freddy and I took to following him and discovered that what he was really doing was taking a belt right out of the bottle. He wasn't ever a falling-down drunk but the real problem with drunks is they become boring. My father became boring, and it didn't become him.

My father died in his sleep of an aneurysm in the spring of

1970, at the age of seventy-seven. By that time my mother had been in a nursing home for several years suffering from Alzheimers. She died a few years after he did. I would have liked to have put my head on that big chest one more time and told him good-bye. He was never a flashy man, and after football, never even a successful man in the way success is measured by historians. He was a good and quiet man, though, filled with common sense and humor.

We never talked about the time we spent working in the woods together. He wasn't like that.

PART TWO

MIND EMPTYING

Ben   As five guys broke into the headquarters of the Democratic National Committee early in the morning on Saturday, June 17, 1972—the story of our generation was beginning, the story that put my *Washington Post* colleagues and me, the executive editor, on the map—I was fast asleep in a log cabin in the hills of West Virginia.

I'd been in the habit of spending weekends in a deserted part of the state's eastern panhandle, chopping down trees and clearing and burning brush on a piece of land I'd bought on the Cacapon River eight years earlier. *Newsweek* had assigned me to cover Jack Kennedy as he traveled to West Virginia in the spring of 1960 in pursuit of a primary win and the presidency. It was early in my career and the work ethic bred into me in the New England woods was my foothold as I climbed the career ladder. It was also getting in the way of my weekends and any opportunity to work in the woods, but that time in West Virginia left a mark in my mind.

It wasn't nostalgia that finally drove me up into those hills five years later. I wasn't yearning sentimentally for Beverly or my childhood or a simpler past. It was simply a taste for the outdoors I had developed as a child.

The log cabin in the woods was called "Seldom Seen," a primitive place a hundred miles from Washington, two miles off a state highway and down a dirt road that was really a riverbed more than occasionally underwater. Overwhelmed in the aftermath of the *Post*'s publication of the Pentagon Papers—and then the many-headed monster that was Watergate, I escaped to West Virginia where I could chop, clear, and burn my way to an empty mind. I could think great thoughts, or no thoughts.

It was a slog up the drive and to the house. Over the years, cars traveling alongside the river had impressed a road, narrowed by cliffs on the right that spilled boulders onto the way. If the Cacapon flooded, different rocks remained and it took a man (usually yours truly and solely) a day to get rid of them. If it rose, I couldn't get in, or out.

By then, chain saws had replaced two-man saws and I'd bought my first Stihl chain saw, patented by a German engineer thirty-odd years earlier as the first gasoline-powered "tree felling machine." I'd be in the woods, chain saw in one hand, ax in the other, by seven-thirty in the morning, scoping the project of the day. The slope in front of the log cabin was my main focus at first:

"Seldom Seen," our original log cabin in West Virginia.

clearing the dead trees from the cabin door to the bottom of the hill, where the river wound by, and keeping the view from the deck clear. It wasn't about a tree here or flowers there.

The land was immense and wild. The work to be done was so close that I'd step out the door and I had a project. It was unmanageable. I could get certain hunks of it but never the whole thing. The goal slipped into the background and the task became more important.

There's a sense of accomplishment from finishing a task. It's sort of silly—trimming a tree is not all that big an accomplishment—but I get the feeling the place looks better if a dead tree is downed, cut into logs, and stacked in the barn. I spend a moment looking back and seeing what I've done, not necessarily as an accomplishment but as a change for the better. You make a piece of ground look better than it was and leave it better than you found it.

I often went alone and worked alone. I don't think of myself as somebody who likes to be lonely and I don't feel it as loneliness. Friends and family would sometimes come to West Virginia and I'd spend the mornings with them before heading off into the hills for some cutting and clearing. The first time I took Sally to West Virginia, I expected she wouldn't like it. I don't associate the woods with Sally Quinn—she's a city girl and a party girl. But she surprised me.

Sally   I never liked the woods. I always thought they were scary. Maybe it was Little Red Riding Hood that did it to me. I just knew there were terrifying creatures that were going to jump out and devour me. Or at the very least, bugs and snakes. I went on one overnight camping trip when I was a Brownie. That was it. I never understood why anyone would choose to be miserably uncomfortable in a sleeping bag instead of snuggling up between crisp sheets, soft pillows, and cozy blankets.

So when Ben told me he had a log cabin on a wild river in the woods in a remote part of the West Virginia mountains, I was apprehensive, to say the least.

The first time he took me there was two months after we had gotten together. We still were seeing each other clandestinely. I was stunned when we first drove down a long dusty road, over a rocky riverbed, and up a hill through the brush to a tiny cabin on a hill, which looked like something out of an old-fashioned movie about Appalachia. It was called "Seldom Seen," the name etched in wood over the door by someone with an ax and a very unsteady hand. Inside the house the walls and all of the furniture were a garish turquoise blue. Somebody had clearly given the previous owners several free cans of paint, and there were a few lumpy chairs and creaky iron beds with worn-out mattresses. This was not what I had had in mind.

But I was in love. When Ben took me down to the river I was sold. What a beautiful, remote, pristine, silent, peaceful place it was. We had the whole world to ourselves. I had just started a job with the *CBS Morning News* as the first network anchorwoman in America. It was a disaster. Ben was in the middle of Watergate. Somehow all of that chaos and stress evaporated and we were left alone in a blissful void, without a care in the world.

The next morning, when he got his chain saw and disappeared into the denseness of the trees, at first I was at a loss for what to do. It was a beautiful late summer day and I wasn't in the mood to read so I decided to take a walk. It changed my life. Suddenly the woods were embracing me; the leaves were just beginning to turn a bit and there was the slightest coolness in the air. The sun was sparkling on the river and through the branches. I found a large pine tree, the ground beneath it covered in needles, and lay down. I don't even know how long I was there but when I got up I felt completely renewed.

Ben was the same way when he came in from his adventures.

At the bend of the Cacapon River, surrounded by nothing but wilderness, there was a chain of lovely smooth, flat rocks that jutted out into the center of the rushing waters. We would meet there for lunch. I would bring a picnic, usually fruit and cheese, bread and wine, and we would sunbathe on the glistening stones for an hour or so before he disappeared back into the trees until dusk. He was always completely refreshed at the end of the day, when he would return from his endeavors covered in grime and usually bleeding from having been cut by some random branch or thorns. After a shower we would sit out on the porch in an old iron rocker and have a drink. He was a different person.

The Cacapon River, as seen from our property.

Ben and his wife had separated earlier that summer. Our relationship became public shortly afterward, but for several months we just wanted to be alone. He got an apartment in the Watergate. (I was still living and working in New York until that December.) But neither one of us could wait until the weekends for our escape to West Virginia and our beloved woods.

Ben   When I'm working, I have the emptiest head you ever saw. I just don't think of anything. I concentrate on the task and try to avoid blades of any kind. When I was in West Virginia during Watergate, I wasn't thinking about the denials and counterattacks coming from the White House, or whether Woodward and Bernstein's sources were reliable, or Nixon's landslide reelection, or our inability then to break new ground in the Watergate story, or Deep Throat's warning for our physical safety. I was thinking about the tree in front of me—where to take it down, how to take it down, what line I would lay it down on. But I was no great artist about it and more than anything working in the woods was an escape because I loved the mind-emptying part of it even though I'm not known for my introspective thoughts.

Sally   The day Nixon resigned was an extraordinary day at the *Post*. Contrary to what one might expect, the atmosphere in the paper was more solemn than gleeful. It finally hit us—all the immensity of what had happened to the country and the enormity of the risks that the paper had taken. Everyone was a bit shell-shocked. I spent the day at the White House covering Nixon's departure on the White House lawn. Surprisingly, I wept when he got on that helicopter and waved that final V-for-victory to the crowd. Rather than just feeling proud for the paper and the work we had done (which I was), I felt terribly sad for the country. It truly was a tragedy.

That night Ben and I didn't want to go home alone. Neither did Kay Graham. We didn't have any plans and Kay asked what we were doing. So the three of us went to Nathan's tavern in Georgetown and had cheeseburgers. No fancy restaurants, no filet mignon, no champagne. Oddly, the last thing we felt like doing was celebrating. Nor did we want to appear as if we were. We were uncharacteristically subdued. The three of us were sort of clinging to each other. Even though I had been covering the Watergate characters for several years, Ben and I had only been with each other for a year. But Ben and Kay had really been through the fires together, risking their reputations, their lives, and the paper. It was sobering.

The next day Ben and I took off for West Virginia. He was desperate to get back to his sanctuary, the woods, which had been his salvation throughout those tough years. We spent the weekend in silence.

Very soon after Nixon resigned, Ben decided he wanted to go to West Virginia to work on a book about his relationship with Jack Kennedy. Ben and his then-wife, Tony, had been the Kennedys' closest friends during their White House years. The four of them had spent the weekend before the president was assassinated together at the Kennedys' farm in Virginia. They were with

Jackie at the hospital the night she got back from Dallas with the president's body. The two of them spent the weekend alone with Jackie shortly afterward. It was Tony who found Jackie's house for her after she moved out of the White House. (Coincidentally, it is directly across the street from the house we now live in.)

At that point Ben and I were engaged to be married. But he wanted to go to West Virginia alone and work on the book. For a month. Needless to say I was not happy about this but I knew he needed that time in the woods to process all that he had been through. He never called me once the whole time he was there. I thought our relationship was over. When he came back he had a graying beard; he was a different person. He told me he still loved me but he wasn't ready to get married. He had never spent that much time alone and he had cherished the experience. Ben doesn't pray, really, but I felt that he had been doing what was his version of praying in the wilds of the mountains. Our relationship became much closer, more intense after that month. I had had time to think, too, while he was gone. I realized that neither one of us was ready for the commitment that we would ultimately make. It was his time with nature, which had once again served to clarify for both of us where we were in our lives together.

Eventually we built a new contemporary house on a rock ledge overlooking the Cacapon River with dramatic views and lots of windows that let in the sunlight. I had loved the cabin but it was dark and impossible to keep clean and the kitchen was hopeless. However, I really did miss the coziness and quaintness of the old cabin. The new house was great but I never really felt at home there.

If you had told me that I would spend my honeymoon weekend in the mountains of West Virginia I would have said you were crazy. Oddly enough though, there was only one place I wanted to be that gorgeous October weekend and it was alone with Ben, overlooking the wild river in the woods. We had had a very quick wedding with

The house we built in West Virginia.

less than a week to plan. (I was afraid he would change his mind.) Ben had been skeptical of getting married and didn't want to tell anyone so we simply invited all of our friends to a dinner party that Friday night without telling them why. (Ben later said he didn't want anyone to know about it because he didn't want to get scooped by our rival paper, the *Evening Star*.) Only our immediate family was there. Ben's best men were Edward Bennett Williams and Art Buchwald (for the second time, as this was Ben's third wedding). My matron of honor was Katharine Graham, who had stopped off at a florist in New York and picked up a bridal bouquet, ribbons and all, and carried it down with her on the shuttle that afternoon.

We were married by Judge David Bazelon in his chambers and then went right to the party. When our guests arrived, there I was in a short white dress, white flowers everywhere, a big wedding cake on the table and champagne for everyone.

The next morning Ben and I piled in the jeep and off we went to Seldom Seen. I just remember thinking that nothing could ever make me happier than I was that day. (Later I had to admit that the day Quinn was born was the happiest day of my life.) The sun was brilliant on the cascading water over the rocks and the moon was out in full that night as we had a cozy fire and planned our life together. It seems that so many of the wonderful and momentous things that have happened to us have been alone in nature. My toast to Ben at our wedding was that the magazines and papers would report that we had been married and that it was "her first, his third." But they would be wrong, I said. They should say it was "her only, his last."

We actually did go to St. Martin at Christmas for our "real" honeymoon. But nothing could ever compare to those two magical days we spent together in the woods.

———

Ben   One day when I was in West Virginia by myself, I went out on the porch of the log cabin. There on the deck was an owl, dead. He had a clothesline rope that he had bit into and had obviously been trying to swallow but had choked on it. That was just the strangest sight I'd ever seen: an owl with a rope in his throat, dead. I always kick myself for not cutting the rope and having the owl stuffed. There's something about the wise owl. He's so damn wise that he swallowed a piece of rope that killed him. I'd like to have that on my desk. Just 'cause you think you're smart enough to do anything, don't go swallowing any rope.

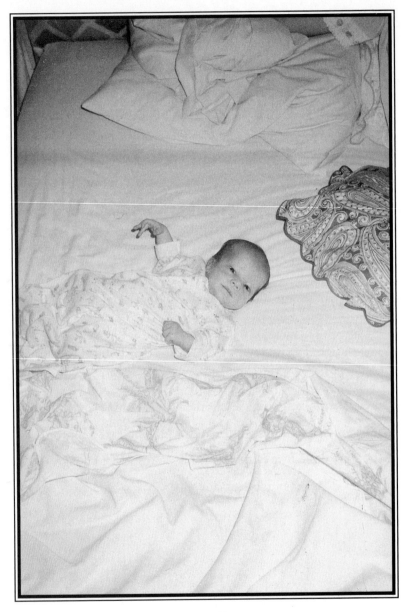

Josiah Quinn Crowninshield Bradlee

QUINN'S ARRIVAL

Ben Our son, Quinn, formally known as Josiah Quinn Crowninshield Bradlee, was born on April 29, 1982, after a long, difficult delivery. For twenty-four hours he lay there with eyes wide open, never crying. When the doctor told us the next day that she had found a heart murmur, we bought into the explanation that many babies have heart murmurs that disappear. But Quinn's didn't, and within weeks the murmur was redefined as a ventricular septal defect, a small hole in one of the chambers of his heart. Blood was pumping through his heart, and through the hole, without getting to the rest of his tiny frame. Quinn struggled to gain weight for weeks until, when he was just barely ten pounds, he began to *lose* weight, and open-heart surgery became urgent.

Sally It was only after we got married in 1978 that I began thinking of having a baby. It took two years to convince Ben, twenty years my senior, who felt that he was too old to be a father again. I always thought I wanted a girl. Despite my lovely walks and my books, there were times when I got lonely in the cabin when Ben was out in the woods. Wouldn't it be wonderful to have a little daughter with whom I could play dolls and dress up and read fairy tales and bake cookies?

When I got pregnant and learned I was having a boy I spent a weekend mourning the loss of my daughter and all those pink frilly clothes—then I began bonding with my son Quinn. I named him right away and held constant conversations with him. We were best friends from the start. He was going to be a miniature Ben and I would simply have to live with the fact that he would have an ax and eventually (I shuddered) a dreaded chain saw and I would have to give him up on the weekends.

Quinn was born in April, three weeks late with a hole in his heart. At first it didn't seem all that serious. It was not uncommon and the doctors reassured us that in most cases the holes close up by themselves by the time the child is two. Ominously, though, they did give us warning signs of heart failure. At first Quinn seemed to thrive and after a month Ben prevailed upon me to take him to West Virginia. We hadn't been there for several months because of my pregnancy and Ben was going crazy without a tree to chop down.

I knew something was wrong even driving out there Saturday morning. Quinn was very fussy and wasn't nursing properly. This was unusual. He was normally such a good-natured baby. When he was born the nurses at the hospital called him "Mr. Mellow" and his pediatrician had said she had never seen such a "breast-oriented" child in her life. Ben loved that. Quinn didn't settle down that afternoon even as I walked him back and forth across the living room trying to comfort him while Ben was outside.

That night I put him down in a tiny crib in an alcove in our bedroom. It was chilly and yet he was so restless he kept pushing off his blanket. I didn't sleep a wink. The next morning he was having trouble breathing and it was clear something was terribly wrong. I began to panic. We left immediately and started to drive back to Washington but he was crying so hard and gasping for breath so desperately that we kept having to pull the car over to walk him around. Finally we stopped at a gas station (there were no cell phones in those days) to call the Children's Hospital cardiologist. When I described his symptoms, the doctor told us to get him to the emergency room immediately because he was probably in heart failure. By that time so was I. We made it back to Children's probably at ninety miles an hour.

Quinn was, in fact, in heart failure. I didn't leave the hospital for two and a half months. They were hoping to postpone the heart surgery until he was stronger but he kept losing weight, and though he was stabilized and nursing it was clear to me that he wasn't going to make it. He was three months old and weighed eight pounds. Finally they decided to operate on an emergency basis. The night before the surgery may have been one of the toughest of my life. Quinn wasn't allowed to have anything to drink after midnight yet every time I would hold him he would go for my breast and when I had to pull away he would start to cry. He was okay when Ben held him, but not with me. It was agonizing.

The next morning, when we had to hand him over to the surgeon, we really didn't think we would ever see him alive again. I literally collapsed and fell to my knees sobbing. Ben, trying to make me feel better, said, "Well, think of it this way. He'll never have to go to war." I hadn't thought of that. But having lived through World War II and Vietnam with a general for a father and later a pacifist brother, it was oddly comforting.

Ben In early July 1982, the same week that Quinn went into heart failure, the *Post* went to trial in a libel case brought against us by the president of Mobil Oil Corporation. He sued the paper for a front-page story describing how he had set up his son as a partner in a shipping management firm that then did millions of dollars in business operating Mobil-owned ships under exclusive, no-bid contracts. We were sure we were going to win.

I've only worked for one company, in effect, in my life. Loyal to whatever cause I'm involved in, I went back and forth between the courtroom and Children's Hospital. I wanted to be in court to show the jury and the judge that I wasn't scared of the case and I wanted to be at the hospital to show my son I was there for him.

I don't remember reaching a time when we thought Quinn was going to die within the next few hours but the prognosis was terrible. I think Sally and I both were subconsciously steeling ourselves for a terrible loss. Late in July, the doctor told us only surgery would save Quinn's life, and so, early in the morning on July 30, 1982, Dr. Frank Midgley operated. I'll never forget that doctor if I live to be a hundred. He had the biggest, kindest hands I ever saw. For those huge hands to hold a tiny scalpel and tie off something inside a little heart seems like an undoable thing.

Just after the operation, we stood over Quinn, who was unconscious inside a plastic oxygen tent. It is the image of Quinn that I will never lose. Sally was on one side, I was on the other, and Quinn lay in the middle, each of his tiny hands holding one of our fingers. He was out but he just kept holding on.

That very day the jury in district court came back with a verdict. I rushed from Quinn's bedside down to the courtroom to hear what we expected—Bradlee and Woodward, not liable—

and what we never expected—the *Washington Post* and reporter Patrick Tyler were found liable. I was stunned.

Sally and I decided to invite the whole team of lawyers and fellow defendants back to the house for drinks and supper that night. We ordered in. I just don't understand why we did it. My feeling, I guess, was that we ought to try to keep everybody's spirits up. And the doctors insisted we get some sleep since Quinn was in the ICU and we couldn't spend the night there.

Early the next morning we were at Quinn's bedside. I was in awe. He just kept going. Why? What is it that drives an infant? We have an expression my father used to say to me—or at least I told it as if my father said it to me: "Nose down, ass up, and push forward." You keep trying. But I never had to fight as Quinn did. I think I cried once over the frustration of not being able to walk when I had polio. But I was much older and I wasn't as sick. I challenge people to find anything wrong with me now that had to do with polio. My little toes are shorter. Big deal.

Quinn healed from the heart operation and began to grow and gain strength. He had eighty-four stitches, like guitar strings back and forth across his chest—from his tally whacker to his throat. Until the incision healed and even immediately after, the scar was very red. I couldn't escape it if I held him in my arms or if I put him in the tub. It grabbed my eyes, to say the least. But remarkably soon after the operation, I began not to worry about him physically. We knew he wasn't going to die from his heart condition, but with him at just a few months old, we didn't know what the ultimate consequences of this disease were going to be. That was one of the biggest challenges and scariest things about Quinn's condition. We knew we were going to get through it, but we still weren't in the clear by any means.

Sally   Quinn recovered from his operation but for months I was too scared to take him to the mountains, so Ben would drive up for the day, work out in the woods, and come home. It wasn't for many months that I felt secure enough to take Quinn.

What I found when I did was that I was stuck in the house all day with a baby and Ben would be out clearing, burning, and chopping. I tried taking a babysitter but because we had no TV reception in those "hollers" they refused to go.

Ben would put Quinn in a Snugli backpack and we would take walks in the woods together and I would do the same with Quinn by myself but it wasn't really satisfying for either of us.

I found we were going less and less and Ben was more unhappy about it. Quinn was sick all the time. He had pneumonia a lot, he developed epilepsy when he was two, he was constantly in the emergency room with seizures, and he was clearly learning disabled. At that point, I never really felt safe with Quinn out there, not close to a hospital. The house wasn't safe, either. It was on several levels and had an open deck where we had to install chicken wire so he wouldn't fall down the rocks. There was no yard where he could play by himself, and there were copperheads, which made me crazy since he loved nothing more than to pick up sticks when we were walking. Ben got him toy axes and plastic chain saws and he would follow Ben out to the woods to play with him but Ben was always afraid he would be hurt and I would have to stay with them. Often Quinn and I would spend weeks in Children's Hospital, after various surgeries or illnesses.

West Virginia wasn't working for us anymore. Ben knew it, too.

I began looking for another country place. The two prerequisites: it had to be on the water and it had to have woods.

A walk in the woods in West Virginia.

ABCs

Ben   By the time Quinn was four years old, we knew his thoughts weren't always consecutive. Somebody would say something and he would apparently join in a conversation but he'd pick it up at a different point. Normally it goes A to B to C, the conclusion. That didn't, and still doesn't, work with Quinn all the time. Sometimes he gives A, then he goes to B, and that should equal C, but to Quinn it equals G. It rattled Sally and me for a while. We could understand what he was saying but he would veer the conversation. Once I spent some time thinking about it, I could work out the logic to it. It always made sense how he got there but he stopped the continuity of what people thought was under discussion and started something else. There was a transition that we wouldn't normally see but that he saw.

That year, we enrolled Quinn in the Lab School, a school for learning-disabled children in Washington, D.C. A woman called Sally Smith was the head of it. She was a tough old blister, yet very good. It was a wonderful school that recognized that some kids are learning disabled to a point where it really influences their life. It's the most important thing in their development and it took me some time to come to grips with that. It was hard for me to think that we had a child who was so different that he required a different education. There was never anyone else close to me who had learning disabilities. I come from a success-oriented culture, though not abnormally so, where kids may have been different, but they weren't far out of the mainstream. Quinn was far out of the mainstream, certainly in the beginning. And I didn't know what it meant. The word *retarded* was always floating around in the room, although never used.

Except once. Sally and I consulted a highly regarded psychiatrist in Washington who testified at various trials as to people's mental capacity. When Quinn was eight years old, we sent him to see her and, after a number of visits and tests and all that, she called us in and handed us a report. In short, it said Quinn was borderline retarded. She suggested that he was going to need to be institutionalized in one way or another. It was an incredible moment. One that we anticipated, but certainly not in those words. But at that point the problem changed. He was going to live but he was going to live a different and difficult life.

I was just crushed. Before I had to confront that, though, I had to confront and comfort Sally. She was devastated, and so was I. I say this about women generally, but if their child is involved, it's a different set of rules. It so overwhelms their thinking.

I was consumed with fixing it. I've always had the great belief in curability: that things will get fixed, or that I can fix things. When I had polio, I knew I would get through it and walk again. There was never any doubt. I think my makeup is so simplistic that once I understood what the task was that lay ahead of me, it was there to be done. It wasn't there to be worried about to death. This report spelled out the dimensions of the problem at hand. It was more clarifying than frightening. In a strange sort of way it was marvelous for me in giving a purpose and focus to my life beyond just having a successful marriage and being there for my son. It made marriage harder but on the other hand, more meaningful.

Years later, when Quinn was fourteen, a title emerged for the problem. VCFS, or velocardiofacial syndrome. I said, "Oh, shit." I studied Latin, so I knew what the words meant, that it had to do with the palate and the heart. There was plainly something wrong with his heart but beyond that I couldn't understand much about VCFS. It is a genetic syndrome that affects about 1 in 2,000 people worldwide, manifesting itself as a range of physical ailments and learning disabilities, which Quinn clearly had.

I kept the psychiatrist's report. It is in my desk drawer at the

Post. I've read it a few times since it was written. I go around futzing for a key or something and I'll see it. She just diagnosed him wrong. He's not retarded. I mean he isn't what she told us he was going to be. And it never seemed right to us.

She plotted a course for him, but not one that we followed.

PART THREE

———

Quinn   My grandfather taught my dad just by being alone sometimes and just by sitting and listening. Our greatest teachers are our ears. Of all things, our ears and then our eyes and then our mind. Our ears come first and he just listened to his dad.

My grandfather taught himself to listen to the trees, to listen to the birds, to the grass even—the sounds of the woods. He got so good he could name every single tree there possibly was and he got to know all the tools and he learned how to fix them.

Probably some of the happiest times my dad ever had with his dad were in the woods. I think my dad wanted me to have that.

Ben, Sally, and Quinn on the beach at Porto Bello

PORTO BELLO

Quinn My favorite place in the world is an old tobacco farm on the St. Mary's River in Maryland that my parents bought when I was a kid. I love to go there whenever I can.

Every time I go to Porto Bello, I feel like I'm there for the first time. There is so much to see and explore. To get there, you turn off the main road and onto a dirt driveway. Sometimes I feel like I'm taking a different path in life when I drive on the dirt road, a path to a place where I can be who I want to be and do what I want to do. Porto Bello is my sanctuary.

The driveway cuts through cornfields until you see trees that carve an outline of the land along the river. The road forks, and to the left there are farm buildings where we park our beat up truck and store our tools. To the right, there are huge trees and the water. I always go that way, past the old cemetery where my dog Sparky is buried next to a couple of people who lived at Porto Bello over the generations.

Porto Bello

Sometimes Porto Bello can get very foggy and gray. It looks like the place in the horror film *The Ring*. But no matter what the weather is, it is absolutely gorgeous. It is one of those places weather cannot ruin. Even when it gets so cold that the whole river freezes, I love it there.

I was only eight years old when my parents bought the place so I don't remember what it was like when we got there, but my dad does.

Ben   My first job after I stepped down from the *Post* editorship in September 1991 was to head the Historic St. Mary's City commission. The "city" is anything but. It is the fourth-oldest settlement in America, founded by Catholics and nestled in St. Mary's County, a lost little province in southern Maryland. It's not on the way to anywhere—you go down there, but you don't go through it, you have to go back up. I got absorbed by St. Mary's City and by the college down there.

Sally heard about the house from friends and drove down looking for it one day. She came back and said, "I just saw a place that you're going to love." We went back that weekend and she was right. Nineteen days later we owned it.

Porto Bello was built by William Hebb II in the 1740s. Hebb had been on a British expedition to Spanish America to avenge a British officer who claimed that his ear was cut off by the Spaniards. When Hebb returned to America he built a house where the St. Mary's River creeps into the Potomac. He called it Porto Bello after the small port town on the Central American isthmus where a battle in the so-called War of Jenkins' Ear was fought.

When we bought the house two hundred fifty years later, the place was a wreck. We lived in the guesthouse for the first year— there was a living room, a bathroom and one bedroom for the three of us. But there were an awful lot of woods and work. There was going to be enough for me to do forever.

Porto Bello is so different from West Virginia because it's so civilized. It's a former tobacco farm accessed by a long driveway, each side lined with corn, wheat, or soybeans planted by a farmer who leases the land from us.

The previous owner had cut down a lot of the trees. They were beautiful walnuts and luckily one of the largest pecan trees in Maryland is still there. But the land had been ignored.

Quinn and I went out and started working in the woods the next weekend. When Quinn was younger, he'd go out and work like hell for about half an hour and then he would find a little rock and be off on a tangent for a couple of hours. He would always find something interesting, whether it was an old brick or a stone. The land was an Indian reservation so there are always arrowheads down there.

Being in the woods with him then allowed me to get to know Quinn. I watched how he would concentrate, what his attention span was, and what diverted his attention. I don't consider myself a patient person but I was able to understand my son a bit more. I'm still not sure I know how Quinn's brain works. I know that at certain times it doesn't act in a way that we think is logical and sometimes his answers and observations seem inappropriate.

Quinn strikes out on his own.

But sooner than I thought, he enjoyed accomplishing whatever task we had, no matter how petty it was. Moving a rock,
carrying a log. He could scamper up trees so sometimes I'd
send him up to cut off a dead limb I couldn't reach. Gradually
Quinn went out more and he loved it, especially when I gave
him the chain saw and he could whack away. I loved that he
liked working in the woods. If Quinn didn't like the woods, we'd
have found something else to do together. It's just very ordinary

sharing that's important. It isn't the top of the mountain; it's the mundane climbing.

When we are together in the woods, it's exactly the way I was with my father. It's quite a silent occupation out there. We focus on the task, which is important. When I think back to Beverly, the tasks were always menial but always important to me. For years I would go up that goddamn driveway and see little places in the woods that I'd neatened up and I'd be proud of the hard work I'd put into it.

At first I was trying to teach Quinn about work. Nothing is too small and it's important to do everything completely. That I got from my dad. Even though he was a big cheese in Boston as a former all-American football player and he brought a considerable reputation with him wherever he went, there was no job too menial for him.

Now I didn't set out for the woods with Quinn with a lesson in mind. I was not conscious that one day I was going to teach him how to do this and the next I was going to teach him how to do that. Whatever the project is we do it together and he, by copying me, learns. When I was with my dad, I never got the feeling that I was getting lessons but I got the feeling that he was teaching me a whole lot of good things. I hope Quinn feels the same way. We don't have an agenda out there, except to be together.

Sally Quinn was eight when we bought Porto Bello, a beautiful eighteenth-century manor house on the St. Mary's River, atop a hill surrounded on three sides by water. It was a complete ruin. The roof had fallen in, two sides were open to the elements, the walls were water damaged nearly beyond repair, a lot of the original moldings were missing, the floors were rotten, the windows all broken, the plumbing nonexistent. The previous owners, descendents of the original owner, had torn off the newer wings and had planned to restore the house to it original size. Unfortunately, they had cut down and sold the hundred-year-old trees surrounding the house. It had been abandoned for over ten years. It looked like a moonscape. But it had two hundred acres of woods. I was in heaven. Ben was in heaven. Quinn was in heaven.

By then Quinn was healthier, though we were still spending large amounts of time at Children's Hospital. He had his first of four throat surgeries that year to improve his speech since he was sometimes hard to understand before then. He was a good swimmer, we had a TV (and Nintendo!), there was a huge yard, we put in a pool, we got a little Boston Whaler (*The Sally Queen*) and it was close to a doctor and a hospital.

That was when Ben and Quinn really began to forge their relationship, because Quinn was beginning to be able to focus on small tasks and all he wanted was to be around his father outdoors.

It took a year to renovate the manor house so we lived in a tiny two-room cottage on the property. Finally we moved into the big house. I immediately staked out the far sunroom, with its fireplace and French doors overlooking the river across the Potomac, all the way to Virginia. Ben and Quinn gravitated to the library, a dark red room with a fireplace and a big TV for watching the games.

That's also when I began to realize how lucky I was to have had a boy. Ben and Quinn would be outside, leaving me to take long walks in the woods alone, read quietly by the fire, or write on my own side of the house. Then they would come inside and settle down in front of the TV to watch sports. Any sports.

Quinn would be good for a few hours working outdoors with Ben, then he would come in to watch a movie or play video games. Their time together was not always working side by side. Quinn showed signs of being an avid archeologist even at a young age and our property is a treasure trove of old objects from arrowheads to stove pipes to pieces of eighteenth-century porcelain and old glass bottles. So when he got bored clearing brush (this was pre–chain saw) he would start digging.

The most interesting thing about the two of them working together was the change in Quinn's relationships with his father and me. Until Quinn was about eight or nine, I had been the principal caretaker in his life. I had taken a leave of absence from the *Post* when he was born and was never able to return to work full-time because of Quinn's health and learning problems. I wrote two novels during that time and an occasional piece for the paper or a magazine but I was pretty much out of commission professionally until he was sixteen. It was then that he went off to a special boarding school for learning-disabled boys, the Gow School, near Buffalo.

Fathers are generally not as good with little children, especially sick little children, as mothers are, and Ben was no exception. Quinn's care and maintenance had been my domain and I would never have had it otherwise. Men are generally not as interested in babies as women are. They really start turning on to kids when they can do things with them.

Suddenly I was faced with losing Quinn on some level. As much as I loved having the two of them disappear into the woods weekend mornings, each time I could feel myself giving up a little piece of him. I was thrilled that Ben was taking a new and different interest in Quinn and that Quinn clearly adored being with his father. I was happy that Quinn was able to achieve a certain independence from me. Still, I have to admit I felt conflicted. The happiest time of my weekends was when Quinn would come in from the woods by himself and snuggle up with me in front of the fire in the sunroom.

SATURDAYS

Quinn   When I was a kid, my dad and I would get up on Saturday morning around nine and my dad would make breakfast. There is a big window beside the stove in the kitchen. When I was little, I'd sit on the windowsill in my OshKosh B'gosh pj's and watch him make breakfast.

If I work it right, he still will make breakfast for me. Not so often anymore, but every once in a while if I walk up to him, hug him, give him a big kiss, and ask, "Will you make your loving son some breakfast?"

My dad makes the best blueberry pancakes in the world. Nobody can make pancakes the way he does. He just does something. I'm afraid to make pancakes. I'm just afraid I'd put in too much milk or water or something.

Ben   It's out of a box. You get pancake flour from a box that says "buckwheat flour pancakes" and put in a little milk and drop an egg in. I do actually add the blueberries. That's very sweet of him, but it's one of my lesser skills.

Quinn   After breakfast we will cruise around looking for projects. My dad loves projects.

Ben   Quinn and I walk around the property or get in the Jeep and drive around and it's a matter of a few minutes before we see something that challenges us to improve it. So we pick a spot and we'll fix it up. It's not supposed to look manicured. I just love going out in the woods and making a piece of ground look better than it was. But I like to have a project. I'm project oriented, and sometimes when I don't have a project I just go out of the house and walk around or drive the Jeep around until I see something that can benefit from a day's work. You know, if there's a dead damn tree sticking right up in the middle of a field and you want to get rid of it, get it out of there.

Quinn   My mom was like a butterfly on the wall then and she loves to talk about our serious planning.

Sally   Ben and Quinn developed rituals. Cooking breakfast was a big deal. They are breakfast freaks. I find breakfast boring. So they would have long discussions about whether it would be pancakes, French toast, scrambled or fried eggs, bacon or sausage. Ben usually cooked but Quinn would help out.

While they were eating breakfast they would plot out their projects for that day. Would they clear the beach of litter so that I could walk it, would they take down the dead tree up by the campfire, would they pull out the vines choking the little island of forest in the center of a field, would they burn their now ten-foot pile of branches in an open patch of land or was it too windy? They were so serious you would have thought they were planning the Normandy landing on D-Day.

Once they had finished breakfast they would put on matching canvas work suits (in the winter, in the summer it was jeans and T-shirts). They would fight over their work gloves, then they would get the keys to the Jeep, and head out to the barn for their axes, pole saws, clippers, and one of Ben's five chain saws. There were always several out being sharpened. That was the thing that terrified me. Ben had strict orders not to let Quinn anywhere near a chain saw. I should have known better.

Quinn   Nature tells us where to go. Sometimes it can be really obvious, like a branch that fell down. When it comes to something like that, it is not only something that has to be done, it is something that looks kind of ugly if you do not do it. If it is just lying there it will look like we are not really taking care of the property and we are not keeping it up.

Other times there might be a small branch that has fallen out of the burn pile and my dad will tell me to go get it. And I will say I was just going to tell you to go get that. But he taught me how to find the places that need to be cleared and how to do it.

Ben   Briars grow like vines. You can't reach them and even if you could they'd cut your arm so you have to go way down at the bottom and cut them with hand clippers. Then you take out this big mare's nest of vines all balled up and start rolling it to the fire pile. It turns out to be the easiest way.

Quinn   One time I saw a deer run through the briars and I felt really sad for it. I was worried it would get cut up from the thorns but my dad told me they actually use the briars to scratch themselves. That's how tough their skin is.

Even just pulling out the briars is satisfying, because I've freed the tree. I get so much pleasure from it. When we get rid of briars and all the other brush, we have a view of the river. It is just such a satisfying feeling.

I think the very first thing we did at the farm was clean up the clearing where there is a gazebo. I found a picture of my dad and me in his Jeep. My dad was driving. I think it was right when we had just moved down there. I must have been eight years old. It's very foggy and my head is just popping up over the windshield. That's where we first started, and then we just kind of moved around.

I remember my mom wanted us to clear the beach so she could walk on it. I spent a couple of years clearing it. It took that long because I'd get distracted by another project. But

Ben and Quinn in the Jeep at Porto Bello.

nothing is ever all cleared in the woods. It will never stop. My dad and I started off in one place and then we went off and explored and when we came back to where we started it was all regrown. In that sense it is a lose-lose situation but that is what makes it so fun. I will never, ever be bored in the woods. Unless you pull the roots out of the ground, there is always something to be done. My grandkids will be working in the woods there, hopefully.

Toys and Tools

Quinn   When my dad first let me use the chain saw, he was terrified. He would not let me use it alone, I remember. My mom was terrified, too, but my dad might have been more terrified because he taught me.

I learned how to use the chain saw over a few days. It is an interesting machine. One of the lessons my father taught me about a chain saw is that you should always be a little afraid of it. I was more nervous than afraid when I first learned to use it. But once you get used to it, it is like once you get used to being with a girl, you get familiar with her. You know all of her ins and outs and when she is going to react badly to certain things. I know they do not like to be compared to machinery, but women are like chain saws. And you have to be focused 100 percent when you are using a chain saw. One slip and you are done. But I am more terrified of women than I am of chain saws.

I like cutting down big trees. It feels like I have power. We won't cut down an entire tree very often but we do every once in a while. It is a great feeling and I love the sounds of a falling tree. I just love the crackling. It is kind of like when you pour milk on a bowl of Rice Krispies.

I think I would love to be a logger and cut down trees that are three hundred feet tall. I'd get to use tractors, bulldozers, machinery, and cranes to lift up the huge trees. The trunks are so big they have to be cut in half first and then finished. And when you're cutting them you have to be careful because they could completely snap or it could bind the saw and then it's stuck. But they don't use little dinky twenty-inch chain saws, they use forty-inch chain saws. I would much rather work outside than inside all day on a computer.

My grandfather taught my dad how to work out in the woods. When we are using the chain saws, my dad will always say that grandpa would have loved a chain saw back then. They used a two-man saw to cut hundred-year-old trees.

It was a really foggy, overcast day when I went out and used the chain saw by myself for the first time. It was about a year after my dad taught me. He and I were out at the big brush pile and I told him that I had a project that I wanted to do. I asked if I could use the chain saw and he said, "Not without me." But I just went out there and used it on my own.

One time my dad's friend was working with us at our house. He was trying to get the chain saw started but he couldn't. I watched him pull on the cord four times, five times, trying to get it started. I wanted to tell him all he had to do was push the chain brake off but I wasn't sure if that was why it wasn't starting. He checked everything and tried a few more times but he just couldn't figure it out so he gave up. I went over, pushed the brake off, switched the lever, and it started. He looked at me in total shock. My dad was there. I think he was really proud of me. He taught me something that I taught someone else.

A lot of the lessons I learn working out in the woods are analogies for life. I know I should be a little afraid of Mother Nature or of a certain tool the way I should be of life. Because as safe as it is and as fun as it is, it could still be dangerous. When you really get familiar with using a chain saw and you think you have got it down cold, the chain can snap or in a second it can cut your arm off. And life is a lot like that as well.

My dad, on the other hand, thinks he's invincible.

Ben   When Quinn and I began working in the woods together, I was worried about hurting him, or getting hurt with him, especially when he started fooling around with the chain saw. Chain saws are very scary and the damage they can do in an instant is unthinkable. Sally would have killed me if something happened to him and I would've done something to myself. But Quinn really wanted to do it. He plainly wanted to help me.

Quinn was running a chain saw when he was nine years old. I showed him how to start it. I'd give him endless lessons about always keeping his hands down when he held the chain saw because it keeps going unless you take your finger off the trigger. It's dangerous to hold the chain saw with your finger on the trigger so you've got to hold it away. Quinn treated the chain saw with reverence and got quite good with it early on. He's very careful and has never had an accident.

Sally One of the most attractive qualities about Ben is that he thinks he is totally invincible. One of the most maddening qualities about Ben is that he thinks he is totally invincible. Happily that quality was not inherited by Quinn. Quinn was sick enough so much of the time and saw so much death at Children's Hospital that he understands the precarious quality of life. You'd think Ben would have, too, having fought in World War II on a destroyer for three years and faced a kamikaze pilot eye to eye. But Ben knows no fear. He also is repulsed by weakness and cowardice. He can't stand whiners or complainers. "Suck it up" might well be his motto in life. How he ever stayed married to me I'll never know.

One of my greatest fears when Quinn was small was that Ben wouldn't understand or accept Quinn's fragility, his illnesses, his handicaps. I was so afraid he would be turned off by Quinn that he would want nothing to do with him. The fact was, though, that Ben admired Quinn more than anyone he ever knew. I realized at some point that it was because Quinn was a fighter, a survivor. Quinn just wouldn't let his health and learning problems get him down. He rarely cried, even when he was scared, or sick or in pain. He faced his adversities with such courage and determination that Ben was in awe. Ben had known what it was like to be handicapped for that short period when he had polio but he had recovered in less than a year. Quinn was looking at problems he would have to face for the rest of his life. He was always optimistic and never once asked, "Why me?" He basically believed what I had told him when he was little, which was that we all have problems, nobody gets a pass, and that he was lucky he was having his when he was young so that he would know how to handle them when he got older. His attitude was, "this is my problem and if you have a problem with that then that's your problem."

Which brings us to the chain saw. Ben had promised me that when he thought Quinn was ready we would discuss it and he would then start letting him use it with close supervision. Well, he didn't. Unbeknownst to me, Quinn had started to use the chain saw when he was around nine or ten. I could never get an honest answer about when, out of either one of them. Even though Ben said he had tried to teach Quinn how dangerous the saws were, I think it was Quinn who really understood the risks involved in using them. Once I found out that Quinn was using the saw I started "dropping in" on them either before or after my walks just to supervise. What I found amazed me. Quinn was the careful one. It was Quinn who was worried about Ben. "Dad," he would say, "don't hold the saw so close to your leg," or "Dad, don't get up on that ladder with a chain saw." Quinn treated the saw with respect. He used to tease me about how he was more afraid of me than the chain saw. Now his fear has expanded to women in general.

When Quinn went away to school at sixteen, both of us were bereft. It meant that I wasn't getting the hugs and kisses I craved so desperately. Ben, too, for that matter. But for Ben, he had lost his buddy in the woods. I had begun to worry about Ben using a chain saw alone. Though incredibly robust and energetic he was seventy-seven. I admonished him many times to be careful but I also managed to wander out where he was working from time to time just to keep an eye on him. I had just left him one afternoon after having caught him on top of a ladder, precariously sawing off a branch with one hand with his chain saw. I made him get down and promise that he wouldn't try anything so stupid again. It wasn't a half hour later that I heard shouts and screams and rushed out of the house to see what had happened. There was Ben, holding a bloodied arm in the filthy T-shirt he had been wearing. Defiant as ever, not one to be, in his words, "pussy whipped," he had waited until I disappeared, climbed right back up the ladder, and tried again to take out the limb. He succeeded all right, only it was *his* limb he nearly sawed off. We jumped in the car after I had managed somewhat to stanch the bleeding with towels and I sped to the hospital about twenty minutes away. We didn't talk. I was frantic. The doctor said he had missed the brachial artery in his arm by a fraction of an inch. If he hadn't, he could have been dead.

Ben   Hours later, after I was sewn up (sixteen stitches) and pronounced able to leave, we got back in the car and again drove in silence. This time, instead of frantic, Sally was seething. Finally she couldn't stand it. She turned to me, as I was resting comfortably heavily medicated and clearly feeling no pain. In a barely controlled rage, her voice quivering, she spoke. "Asshole!" was all she had to say. She was right.

Sally says I've got a pistol grip when I carry the chain saw in my hand. I think I'm getting a little old for chain saws. I don't know what the hell I'm doing out there at almost eighty-nine anyway. But I enjoy it a lot.

Quinn Thank God, I wasn't there that day. I would have been terrified. Some people just need to learn the hard way. I guess they think, "Well it happened once, it will not happen again." Maybe when you get to a certain age, it does not matter how many times it happens to you, you just kind of ignore it.

My dad does not want me to have a Jet-Ski, and I say, "Well, why do you not want me to have a Jet-Ski?" He says, "Well, because they are dangerous and people get hurt all the time." I say, "Well, that is why I do not want you to use a chain saw." Sometimes it is just not worth arguing. You can save some breath that way. But he is eighty-eight, and an eighty-eight-year-old should not really be using a chain saw, if you ask me.

FRIENDS

Quinn   One of the hardest things for me to do growing up was to make friends, so I spent my childhood with my parents and their friends. My mom thinks that is why my dad and I are so close.

Sally   Probably one of the hardest things for any parent to face is that their children have no friends. There is not a parent with a learning disabled child who has not walked into the lunch room and seen their son or daughter sitting alone eating while other tables are full of happy laughing children. It is heartbreaking. Even though Quinn was at the Lab School of Washington, a coed school for the learning disabled, he had few friends. The kids were all scattered from different parts of the city and Maryland and Virginia, and even if they liked each other they had no way to get together on weekends. Socialization skills are minimal at an early age. He was essentially an only child (Ben had grown children from other marriages who didn't live nearby) and therefore spent a lot of time alone. Ben and I were his only friends. He depended entirely on us for friendship and companionship, not to mention love. While other children were having playdates and going to soccer matches and birthday parties, Quinn was always left out. So we went to the country. We made it seem as if that was what everyone did. I don't think he realized for a long time that there were lots of activities going on in which he wasn't included.

In the end it may have been a blessing. I think Ben and Quinn would never have been as close as they were had it not been for the fact that the three of us were alone together on weekends. Certainly I was close to him, since I was at home with him every day, but not Ben.

Quinn   I've made a few friends over the years but most of them don't see the point in working in the woods. They are city slickers and they do not want to get dirty. But one of my best friends, Teddy, works out in the woods with his dad, Bo. My dad and I will sometimes go to their farm and the four of us will work together.

One time Teddy was trying to cut a tree root out with an ax. I said, "Nobody's used an ax to cut a root out for a hundred years. Just use the chain saw." He told me he thought it'd dull it up too much. I said, "You know you can sharpen it." There was a long pause and then Teddy said, "It's between me and the root." I know that doesn't really make sense but that's kind of what I like about being in the woods with my friends. It doesn't have to make sense.

History Lessons

Quinn I think my dad was aware that because he is older I was going to spend most of my life without a father so he wanted to spend as much time as he possibly could with me and teach me things. His education to me was teaching me about life in the woods.

Now, I am teaching my dad a lot, too. I'll tell him about cars or about the family history on both sides. I always remind him that the Quinns are from Ireland and he will say he doesn't think of my mom as Irish. Quinn is a patriotic Irish name. It is like Sullivan. Irish Americans take great pride in their Irish ancestry and always have. And that is something that I will never ever stop talking about. But my dad's family are Boston WASPs and everyone knows that history.

My mom's dad, General William Wilson Quinn, or "Dandy" to me, was in the army for a total of thirty-two years. He served in Germany during World War II, where he had a distinguished career as one of the top intelligence officers in Europe, capturing

Hermann Goering, Hitler's most trusted advisor. He also helped liberate the concentration camp Dachau in 1945. As a much decorated soldier, he later fought in Korea. In that war, Dandy was the commanding officer of the famous 17th infantry regiment, and was known as "Buffalo Bill."

I was pretty close to my grandfather. I would go and stay with him and my grandmother twice a week when I was little. My grandfather never really talked about the wars. I know so much more about the history of the war now than I did back then. I wish I had been older then so I could've asked him about the wars.

Dandy and I used to play Yankees and Rebels in his study. That was my only history lesson from him, with little army men. I would be the Rebels and I'd make him be the Yankees, which pissed him off. He loved the Rebels. He was from southern Maryland. General Lee was his hero and he had a picture of him hanging above his desk.

When he died, he left me his jeep and his saber. Every time I get into the jeep, I see the three stars that are on the door because of his rank and I think of him. One of the last times I was with him, he went for a ride in the jeep with me. I was driving and it was a really bad ride. Every little bump he would curse because there are no shocks at all on that thing and it hurt his back. He was a great friend to me and he liked me a lot.

I never met my dad's dad, Frederick Josiah Bradlee, Jr. But I've always been so proud of him. He wasn't a war hero or anything like that but he is a hero in the sense that he went from everything to nothing overnight. After he lost everything in the Depression, he sometimes worked three odd jobs and he even helped run a sawmill. He was a big guy with a big personality and by big personality I mean when things needed to get done, he did it. He'd say, "If that's what I have to do, then that's what I'm going to do." My dad's a lot like that, too.

My grandfather was an extremely smart person and he had a lot of common sense. Whenever his friends would get in trouble, they would always come to him and ask for help. He didn't have any money, but he'd give them advice if they got in trouble.

Every once in a while my dad will tell me stories about his dad if I ask him. My grandfather loved fixing antique furniture. He would hate to see a piece of beautiful furniture in bad shape, so he would ask a friend to buy it and he would fix it up for him. Turns out he was into genealogy and he did a lot of research on our family.

Ben Like Quinn, my dad was obsessed with genealogy. He left us some raw material about our family trees. It seems to me to be interesting to a point, but, on the other hand, people get remote so fast. Quinn got interested in our tree because my mother and father were fourth cousins. The common ancestor Crowninshield was the great-great-great-grandfather of both my mother and father. He was called Benjamin and that's how I got my name. Sounds a little ingrown but it's so far back it doesn't matter.

I think Quinn sometimes gets upset that he broke the Bradlees' Harvard streak. But who cares? I have no problem with that. My sister never went to college. My brother went for twenty minutes. I wish Quinn would be proud of what he's overcome, and he is. His triumphs are real triumphs.

When I was out in the woods with Quinn when he was really young, I had this wonderful sense of pride, especially after that start. We really thought he might not live. I look at him every so often now and it's stunning that he arrived at this point in his life in the shape he's in. And I'm extremely proud of the extraordinary job he's done overcoming his disabilities.

COMMON INTERESTS

Quinn   I love finding out the origins of things. St. Mary's City has a lot of firsts: the first coffeehouse (I'm a big coffee drinker), the first voting rights for blacks and women, and it was the first place in America where a Catholic church was built and where multiple religions were practiced in the same place.

One summer in Maryland I participated in an archeology field school program in Historic St. Mary's City. My dad was chairman of the city commission at the same time. I spent most of the summer excavating an old printing house from the late seventeenth century at the St. John's site. We were mainly looking for pipe stems from old tobacco pipes that the settlers used. I found a couple of clay stems. Some of them are thinner than others and the thinner they are the newer they are. It's very rare that you find the bowls because they break so easily. It's absolutely amazing to hold something that somebody else held three hundred years ago. Probably the coolest and most important thing I ever found was a Calvert coin from 1647. Then, of course, the next day somebody finds another coin. But I found the first coin of the year.

I got so interested I started doing my own little digs at Porto Bello. It's kind of hard to do without all the tools but I just go around and look for places to dig. Les, our caretaker, would tell me where he found artifacts, mostly on the hill where the ground rises a bit. I make a square, remove the topsoil, and then just start digging a little bit at a time with my trowel. Every once in a while we'll be driving around the property and you'll see a giant hole in the field where I've been digging. One of the reasons why I love it is the same reason why I hate it so much as well: you get so dirty. You really get your hands in the dirt and you feel the earth and what's holding us in. I haven't found much, just some arrowheads, some old porcelain, and bottles that we have above the fireplace in the house, but I have a great time.

Archeology is a lot like journalism. It's digging up the layers in time of the earth to find out what happened in history. It's digging up the facts about what happened so you can get a good story.

My dad never did digs with me but he always asked me about what we were finding. The archeologists would do their job and then when they found something important, they would call my dad and he would go over there and check it out.

I don't think fathers and sons have to have the same interests. Of all things, my dad was really drawn to the bindings of books. He thought they were beautiful and he could tell which ones were made by which binder and how and when. A bookbinder is kind of like a jeweler. My grandfather was into it, too. That's something I've never really been interested in. I'm so scared of books as it is. And I think if fathers and sons have close relationships then they don't have to have everything in common.

TOLERANCE

Quinn I think my dad admired my grandfather the most for how he handled my uncle. Freddy was gay and back then people would handle it so differently than they do now. My dad says he will never forget how amazing my grandfather was with him.

I met Freddy a few times. He just loved everybody. He was a kindhearted soul and very British, very proper. He almost had a British accent, for no reason, that's how proper he was. I wish I'd known him more and was closer to him. But from day one, I felt a connection to him. I knew that he was different and he knew that I was different.

My mom says my dad never really had a lot of patience. I think my uncle made my dad a little bit more of an understanding person, more open-minded. Then I came along and I did the same thing for him. My uncle and I were my father's teachers for life and I think if it weren't for us my dad would be a much different person.

Ben   Once an okay athlete, there was no hope I'd become a really good one after I had polio. At school, I turned to debating, editing—even acting—and, for the first time, found myself in the company of outsiders. People like my brother, who at barely nineteen opened on Broadway as Montgomery Clift's understudy in *Dame Nature.* Freddy and I grew apart as teenagers, but I came to understand him a bit more after I had polio and my interests shifted. Freddy was definitely an outsider and Quinn was in many ways, too. I learned a lot about tolerance from both of them. I don't think either of them did it consciously, nor did I accept it consciously as a gift. It was just a benefit that I've gotten from knowing both of them.

Sally   After Watergate when Ben went out in the woods with Quinn, he changed a lot during those years. Here was the "killer" Watergate editor, "the giant slayer," the one who "did not suffer fools," the one who reportedly would "kick anybody over the edge of the cliff for a story," the "most powerful" and "most feared" (I'm quoting from stories) being so patient and understanding and kind to this child, who had had so many problems. Ben treated him like an equal. He made him seem like he was his best friend (as it turned out he was and is). He gave him confidence and a sense of accomplishment at what he could do. He taught him so much, not just about how to cut down a tree or wield an ax, or use a chain saw but about life, about values and morals and perseverance and getting the job done.

Quinn   I've become much more open-minded about people because of the family that I come from. If someone has a sickness and I see they have a sickness, I don't think, "Oh, they'll never be able to do anything." People are just people. They're just trying to get along in the world. You shouldn't treat anybody differently because of what they look like. My dad learned this from his dad, from Freddy, and from me.

FATHERS AND SONS

Quinn Father-and-son relationships are a life's work. There is nothing quite like the bond between a father and son. It is like a two-man saw because in order to start, one of you has to push it, and that's your dad. And then you have to pull it and eventually after you pull it back and forth, you get its momentum going. It's a way of working together when you have to go back and forth and sometimes the saw gets stuck and you're going to have to wiggle it to get it a little loose and then to find where you were.

I think sons and fathers are obviously a little different than sons and mothers. Sons absolutely love their mothers. They love their fathers, too, but it is a different kind of relationship. You come out of your mother's womb literally connected and that umbilical cord is a way you'll always be part of your mother. I think everybody feels a little distant from his or her father subconsciously and that's why we're all drawn to our fathers and why our fathers are so interesting. What makes a father a father? Is a father somebody who raises you or somebody who loves you? I think it's being there from day one and loving your child. It's about love and respect for one another; that is what makes a father a father. It's communion in a way.

A lot of times in the woods we can communicate just through our eyes. I can be riding with my dad in his truck and we can both be thinking the exact same thing. We do not have to say anything. We just look at each other. Sons and fathers can just be near each other and they can almost feel what the other is thinking.

A Place to Fail

Quinn   Nature doesn't have to care about you, but you have to care about it. In a way, I love that. I absolutely love caring for something that can tell me I am doing something wrong in its own way, without breathing down my neck. Nature lets me figure out what I am doing wrong. That's what parents are supposed to do but when you have a loving parent who takes care of their child they sometimes don't let you make mistakes.

If I could change anything about my life it would be my mom letting me fail. She was just too afraid to let me fail. I think my dad is a little bit the same way but he is more laid-back than my mom. Moms are always going to be more cautious about their children.

Sally   Often schools with young learning-disabled children will not encourage team sports. The children have real difficulties being competitive. They don't understand that losing a game means just that. They think if you lose a game it means you are a loser. For Quinn it was even more difficult. Though he was a very good tennis player he stopped because he said he didn't like doing anything where somebody had to lose. He said it hurt him to see somebody lose. This is why even today his favorite sports are individual sports like surfing and snowboarding. One of the great things about working out in the woods for a child who is learning disabled is that there is no competition. The two-man saw is a perfect metaphor for that. You're working together, accomplishing something together, and nobody has to lose.

Quinn   I think the woods are a place where I can fail. Failure in the woods can be quite painful. It is all about safety. Once I was by myself clearing a trail for my four-wheeler and there was a tree that had fallen over and was pinned down by something. The stump was about two feet tall and the rest of the tree was bent down to the ground at a right angle. I started cutting the tree from the top and I cut it right until I got just about halfway to the stump. Then it swung flying upward and just missed my face. I guess if I had started cutting it farther down near the stump it wouldn't have flung up. Trees are sometimes not as friendly as they appear. We tend to forget that trees are living creatures. Just because they do not move, or talk, or oink does not mean that they are not alive. Working out in the woods is life at your own risk.

Ben Success in the woods is measured only in finally cutting the tree down. There are a lot of steps and you don't do all of them perfectly. By that definition, I fail all the time in the woods. There is a tree I should have taken down or a limb I should have cut off that is still there. But for Quinn, he's not being tested every twenty minutes. And unless you are cutting down a tree and rushing to avoid it crushing you, there's no test that is terribly important.

I worry about making mistakes and I often do. Last summer I took down a tree that I shouldn't have. I thought it intruded on the view of the water. I told Sally I was going to do it, and she shrugged as if she didn't object. What I should've done was trim it a little, but I took it down. A few weeks later I realized the view hadn't improved and I hadn't even finished cutting it down.

I certainly don't think profoundly about cutting down a tree before I do it. But life is full of choices. Sometimes you make the right one and sometimes you don't. I'm not conscious of lessons that I learn when I'm learning them and I don't fret about the mistakes I made. There's nothing I can do about it. I can't put the tree back up and there's such an embarrassment of riches in the woods that if you make a mistake, you're soon diverted into all the non-mistakes that are around.

I've always encouraged Quinn to make his own decisions. In

the dynamics of Sally's and my relationship, I have always been pushing him. Let him do it himself, let him work it out. He's got to learn to do this. Sally is always reluctant to come down that path and is always ready to bail him out. I always ask myself: Am I putting obstacles in his way or actually helping him in the long run?

Quinn   There was a willow tree along the water that looked like it was starting to die a little bit and my dad said he thought we should cut it down. I told him it would be a mistake. But he said, "It is dying and it is going to die, so I cut it down." Then he felt so bad.

Sally   When we first moved to Porto Bello we planted a small weeping willow tree on the beach down the slope from the front of the house. We had a beautiful wide covered porch with rocking chairs on it and in the evenings we would sit outside with a bottle of wine, Quinn roughhousing in the grass with his beloved dog Sparky (who is now buried there in the cemetery), and marvel over the spectacular view and watch our little willow grow bigger and more beautiful every year.

Suddenly last spring and summer several of the branches began to die. The tree was so gorgeous, and by then twenty years old, that

Best friends.

I was heartbroken. Ben and Quinn decided to try to prune the tree of the dead branches. They worked for several days and were not satisfied with the way it looked. They both felt it was a bit lopsided. I didn't mind it. Thus ensued many evenings with the three of us on the porch in the rocking chairs, looking across the Potomac at sunset, fortified with Pinot Grigio debating whether or not to take down the willow. I voted no. Quinn felt that we should give the willow a chance, that maybe there had been blight or something and that it would come back. Ben voted to take it down.

So one day when I went out for a walk, they took it down. Not only did they take it down, they had somebody photograph them taking it down, Quinn standing on the stump with his arms raised in a victory sign.

Now, when we sat on the porch, we looked at this big empty space where our precious willow had been and it was sad. Strangely enough, though, I wasn't angry. Quinn apologized to me and said that he had gotten carried away with the project and since then, looking at that gap, he felt it had been the wrong thing to do. The

Momentarily triumphant

amazing thing was that Ben apologized. "I made a mistake," he said. "I should never have cut it down. But I can't put it back up. You learn in life that you make mistakes and you just move on."

The three of us rocked back and forth in our chairs, sipping our wine and contemplating in silence what Ben had just said.

"Well," said Quinn, "we'll just have to plant another one."

And so we have.

Now Quinn will be able to watch it grow and maybe one day his children will cut that one down, too. And plant another.

THE LABYRINTH

Sally: Ben has said himself that he's not very introspective. That's true. He would never describe himself as a spiritual person. Words like that make him uncomfortable. Still, I don't think he realizes how much he actually gets out of working in the woods. I see it as a form of meditation for him. He calls it "mind emptying." No matter how he wants to describe it, what he does out there takes him to a different place.

As for me, I loved my contemplative walks in the woods and the quiet of being alone. There was something missing, though. I felt I needed a place of my own, in a way, just as Ben and Quinn had the bonfires where they could simply be still together and stare into the flames. I had been to a health spa in California years earlier and had been introduced to the labyrinth. It is a flat surface, a maze of sorts, though you don't get lost in it but walk right into the center. It's a meditative tool. The most popular ones are modeled after the one on the floor of Chartres cathedral in France. About six or seven years ago I asked Ben for one for Christmas and he hired the man who had built the one at Grace Cathedral in San Francisco to come to Porto Bello and build one for me. It's fifty feet in diameter and sits atop a small hill at the edge of the woods overlooking the St. Mary's River. It was built on Indian sacred ground. When you approach it from the bottom of the slope you can actually feel the vibrations. Sometimes I think I might actually levitate they are so strong. I walk it every day that I'm there and always come away with some sense of clarity that I didn't have before. Part of what makes it so magical is that it is so private, so close to the forest that you can hear the breeze rustle the leaves and yet open enough so that the sun pours down on you. There is always the sound of the water lapping up onto the beach and the birds and butterflies are everywhere.

I had had two experiences with the labyrinth in California that made me into a total convert. The first time I walked it I was skeptical, especially when I was told that it would change my life. At that time Quinn was very young, had had many medical problems, and was very learning disabled. We had been told that he would never go to high school, much less college, never have friends, never have a job or a relationship or essentially a life. We were even told by some experts that he should be institutionalized. As you can imagine, I was crushed. Shortly after that I went

to the spa and walked the labyrinth. It is situated on a hill surrounded by live oak trees and on this particular day it was brilliant and sunny. I walked to the center meditating about Quinn.
How could I deal with this. I felt so helpless. When I got to the
center I stood for a long time, almost in a trance. Finally I looked
around me and right in front of my face was the most beautiful
palm tree I had ever seen, with a large strong trunk and gorgeous
fronds that stretched out across the labyrinth as if to embrace
everything and everyone around it. Suddenly it became clear to
me what the message was. Quinn was like the palm tree. He was
different from all the other trees but he was far more beautiful. I
felt totally uplifted. When I came back to Washington I realized
that the doctor who had diagnosed him was completely wrong. I
was right.

The next year I went to the same spa and walked it again. It
was the week Quinn was supposed to have major cognitive testing at Children's Hospital, where we had spent so much time.
They had changed the date of the testing but Ben convinced me
to go to California anyway, rightly pointing out that there was
nothing I could do and Quinn didn't even understand what was
going on. I decided to walk the labyrinth at the exact same moment as he was starting his test and I sat in the center of the
labyrinth meditating on him that whole hour. When we got back

and were called in for the results, the doctors looked grim. They were sorry to tell us that he had scored very badly on the tests. Except for one, they said. He had scored higher on this one test than anyone they had ever tested before. It was the maze.

When my labyrinth was finished I had a dedication ceremony with a lot of my friends on my birthday weekend in July. Everyone dressed all in white, drank champagne, and with drumming in the background, filed up to the labyrinth, which was surrounded by candles, and walked it in the moonlight. It was breathtaking.

Now, when I work out in the woods, this is where I work. I clear brush and cut down dead branches with my little blue-flowered work gloves, my clippers, a pole saw, and my chain saw. I've made it so beautiful that now Ben and Quinn will come up to help me out with the heavy-duty work that I can't manage.

Ben doesn't really understand the labyrinth. He's done it once. He walked the winding path slowly into the middle as he had watched me do, stood there for a minute, and then, without retracing his steps, he simply stalked across the circle and out of the space. When I asked him how it was he said, "I don't get it." Quinn was different. He is a spiritual soul. He really liked walking the labyrinth and particularly loved the idea of meditating once he had reached the rose-shaped center. He doesn't do it often but he appreciates what it signifies. Many of my friends have given me tokens to bury amid the river stones that surround the labyrinth. Quinn gave me a tiny crystal rose. Ben gave me a love letter. A portion of my mother's ashes are buried there, too. The most important thing to me is that they both sense what I already know, that it truly is a sacred space. They have theirs. This is mine.

Quinn Chopping wood is a lot like praying to me. It is very congregational. It has a lot of meaning to it. When I am in the woods alone now, I almost feel that my father is with me. I am with my dad. I think because I've learned so much about the woods from him, the woods remind me of my father. Then when I am cutting wood, I feel like I'm chopping away at pieces of knowledge that he has taught me and I'm taking them with me.

ALONE IN THE WOODS

Quinn   My dad and I are like wolves. When we are out in the woods, we are together, and sometimes when we are not, we are like lone wolves. We just go our own ways.

People can only tell you so much. There's a point where you've got to go out and see it for yourself, feel it, do it, and hear it. One of the most relaxing things to me is just sitting out in the woods alone, watching the trees sway back and forth in the wind and just listening to them.

Working in the woods can be very emotional. There have been really bad days when I'd be working by myself and then all of a sudden an eagle would fly over. I almost believe that somebody is watching over me. We have ospreys down there, which are almost as beautiful as eagles, and blue herons, a more feminine bird with long legs and feet that kind of hook in. They fly an inch over the water. It is absolutely amazing to watch. All of a sudden it goes from being really crappy to the best day in the world, at least for me.

CHROMOSOMES
AND THE WOODS

Quinn Les was our caretaker at the farm. He passed away last year. He was an old rebel guy who had Confederate flags in the barn and he was an extremely superstitious guy and very southern. Once my mom told him she wanted to get gloves with flowers on them and her own little clippers. So Les went out to the hardware store in southern Maryland, where there are chain saws and bulldozers, and bought these dinky little flower gloves and these pink clippers for my mom. He said he was so embarrassed because everybody else was buying chain saws and whatnot. And here is this guy with leathery hands and bruises everywhere. My mom actually used them. She went out with the little flower gloves and started pruning. My dad and I were just laughing. He loved it. Every once in a while she goes out and says this or that needs some pruning and I say, "Mom, why don't you get your gloves and clippers and do it?" She is this woods woman now.

Sally I'm like Ben's mother, Josephine. I got the bug. There is something so compelling about watching the two of them working out in the woods together. Sometimes I feel jealous and I want to be part of this bonding thing as well. They both have their big leather work gloves. I have a beautiful pair of blue and white flowered work gloves. That way I can join them when they're out at one of their projects. I love clearing the beach of old dead branches, cutting down small brush that hampers the views, and especially throwing wood on their big bonfires. I think they like to have me visit them from time to time but I'm afraid I have a tendency to get a bit bossy. Why don't you cut down that dead tree over there, or this needs clearing here, or can you take out that vine there. I get the feeling that they're always glad to see me go. They have their own projects in mind and they don't want my interference.

I finally got my own chain saw—a ladies' saw that is lightweight, battery-operated, and cuts like a dream. Now I can take on my own little projects without having to ask them to do it for me. They think it's a riot. They thought the gloves were funny enough. But Mom with a chain saw! Too much. They shouldn't laugh too soon.

Quinn Last summer my mom finally got her pink chain saw. She'd been asking for one for years. It's battery-powered and looks like a little boy's chain saw. But it cuts small trees. The chain

Ben, Sally, and Quinn with chain saws

saw stops completely when you're done cutting with it so it is safe. Now she wants me to paint flowers on it for her.

But the woods belong to the boys. Our farm is the one place where my dad can do what he wants to do. We have our little boundaries that my mom sets about where to go and where not to go. She gets the front of the house and we get everywhere else.

My poor father. I have much more respect for him now that I'm engaged. My dad would get so upset by some things that I just would not understand and now I totally understand.

I remember going to the greenery once with my dad when I was about sixteen. We picked out a lot of azaleas, then my dad put them in front of the house. I think it annoyed my mother because the rule was my mom got the front of the house and my dad got the rest.

Sally   My idea for Porto Bello was to renovate it exactly as it would have been at the time it was built in 1740, plus two additions with more windows that looked as if they had always been there. I decorated the house myself with antiques from that period, historic fabrics, old maps and artifacts found on the property. I wanted only plants and trees that would have been indigenous to the area during that period so we hired a landscaper out of Annapolis who is well-known for designing period gardens. They did a wonderful job. Then Ben suddenly got the mistaken idea that the interior of the house was my domain but that he would make all the decisions about the out-of-doors and the landscaping. (Quinn would inherit his father's sense of propriety over the property, much to my dismay, although I have to say it did contribute to their male bonding. Us against Mom.) This of course was not acceptable. As I pointed out to Ben and Quinn, I didn't suddenly lose my eyesight when I walked out the front door. But Ben seemed determined and of course my balking only encouraged him and Quinn more.

One particular episode was what Ben now refers to as "the bloody azaleas." The three of us were driving down to the country one weekend when we passed a guy on the road with a flatbed truck loaded down with about five hundred azalea plants. They were the most garish fuschia color you have ever seen. Ben slammed on the brakes, pulled over, and asked the guy how much he wanted for the azaleas. Several thousand dollars was his reply. Ben said he would take them, at which point I got out of the car and explained to the nice man that we were in fact not going to take them. Ben looked like a thundercloud so I told Ben through gritted teeth that we would go home and discuss it. The man, clearly not stupid, mumbled something to Ben about how I wouldn't allow him to buy them. On the way to the house, I explained to Ben that we had already spent quite enough on landscaping, that azaleas would not fit in with our scheme, and furthermore, that they were absolutely hideous. Quinn, of course, sided with his dad. Ben didn't say another word. That made me nervous. The next weekend I heard a loud rumble and a dust cloud coming down the road. As it got closer I realized it was the guy in the flatbed truck filled with the five hundred azaleas. He got out of the truck and began unloading them. I rushed over as Ben went to meet him. "What is going on?" I demanded to know. "Your husband bought these azaleas," he said with a huge grin on his face. Ben wouldn't look at me.

As it turned out, this was almost as bloody as the chain-saw massacre. Ben finally gave them as a gift to St. Mary's College, across the river. He kept a few, which ended up behind the fence in his little work cottage where they couldn't be seen. To show he would not be pushed around by a woman, he defiantly planted two of them by the wrought-iron fence next to the little grave-yard where all of the ancestors of the original owner are buried. By the time you read this I will have cut them down.

We had a lovely half-mile-long hedgerow at the entrance to Porto Bello, so that when you got to the end and the road curved to the left you could suddenly see the property, the river, and the barns. It was a wonderful surprise. I especially loved the hedge-row with its pine trees, maples, wild dogwoods, holly, and vines in the fall when they would turn all sorts of shades of orange and magenta and gold.

We lease some of our fields to a farmer to plant corn and soybeans and one day the farmer said he needed a ditch so that the water could run off the field. He wanted to cut down the hedgerow. I said that was simply out of the question. We were not going to cut it down. Ben and I argued about it for months. You can guess where I'm going here. There was one long stretch of time when we didn't come down to the country for several weeks. The next time we arrived . . . no hedgerow. The entire half mile had been completely cut down and there was not a trace of a twig or a leaf left. I went berserk. It took us two months to make up. He wasn't sorry he cut down the hedgerow, he was sorry that he had to bear the consequences. Then I finally asked him if it was worth it. "Yes," he said. "I knew you'd come around." Actually I had followed Ben's advice to "pick your fights." I'd save my ammunition for something more significant than the hedgerow. Like, for instance, the azaleas.

Here's the thing that drives me crazy about Ben and Quinn, particularly when an azalea-type issue arises: they really don't care about gardening. Of course, they like pretty flowers and beautiful gardens, but they have absolutely zero interest in doing it. What they like is the big picture. Flowers are too ephemeral for them. They bloom and then they die. It's not really that they think of gardening as being "prissy," as Ben once said. It's just that they like trees. Big trees. They like cutting down dead trees and sawing them up into logs. They like planting trees and watching them grow over the years. They like clearing brush and cutting down vines and weeds that are choking the trees. They love pruning trees. They both have likened trees to people. Quinn will look at our old walnut tree or the pecan tree, which is the oldest in Maryland, and liken it to his father. When he cuts dead branches off those trees he does it lovingly and with tremendous care, almost as if he were dealing with Ben. Likewise, Ben sees these young trees we planted when we first moved there twenty years ago grow strong and tall and healthy and sees Quinn in them. Their dealing with the trees truly is a life's work for them.

BURNING

Sally   I think Ben and Quinn may be latent pyromaniacs. They are obsessed with fires. The good news is that as soon is there is a nip in the air we have wonderful cozy blazes going in all of the fireplaces in the house. The bad news is that outside they can get out of control. In fact, every morning at breakfast, when they are discussing their projects for the day, the first question they ask is, can we burn today? If it's too windy or too dry the answer is no. Obviously if it's pouring rain that rules it out. They have a huge pile of dead branches and other debris out in the middle of the field at the ready the minute it looks like the conditions are right. Interestingly, it is Quinn who is the more reluctant to burn, even though he loves it. He was there at Porto Bello when he was much younger when the fire caught some dry grass and scorched an entire field. Though he and Ben and a friend desperately tried to control it, the fire department finally had to be called. I'm so aware of their bent on burning that every morning when I come down and hear them planning their day, I will immediately say, "It's not a good day for burning." That's all Ben needs to hear for him to light a match. When will I ever learn!

Happily, Quinn now backs me up. He sees Ben getting older and less able to handle an emergency and he wants to protect him. Recently, when Quinn was not there, and I had gone for a walk, Ben was burning alone. The fire again caught dry grass and in a flash the field was in flames. Ben tried to stop it himself but

The pyromaniacs

got terribly winded and had to call for help. The first I knew of it, I was coming back up the road, only to see several fire trucks circled around what was the original fire. My heart sank. But as I got closer I saw that all of the firemen were talking and laughing with Ben. The fire had been put out and everyone was enjoying a beer. We have the greatest fire department in the world right down the road from us, thank God. Nobody seemed the worse for wear and the blackened grass looked almost new several weeks later. Ben has now promised never to burn alone. We'll see.

Ben Burning is big for me. I love it. I can remember where I got the log that I'm putting on the fire from—what tree and where. I remember cutting it.

Fires have gotten away from me twice and I had to call the fire department. We burn the brush pile in the middle of a field and then it escapes and goes across the whole meadow. It's very scary when a fire gets out of control but more than anything it makes me look like such a fool. One time I was burning some brush by myself. I thought I could control the perimeter of the fire, but it was too big. I called the local volunteer fire company and admitted embarrassingly, "I've done it again." They come with a jeep equipped with a little tank and hose. It's more of an exploratory mission than an all-out fire call and, once the fire is in check, the firemen start squirting each other and just have a good time.

But the healing quality of nature is amazing. Three weeks after that happened, you couldn't see any sign of it.

Quinn Sometimes I will be in the mood for cutting wood, sometimes I will be in the mood for burning. But I love watching a fire that I've made, especially on a cold southern Maryland day.

My dad and I will be working out in the woods and we will throw all the brush into one side of the bed of his truck and all the larger logs on the other side. Then we'll bring all the brush to a bonfire pile that we have in a big field. The bonfire is just a big-ass fire. The piles would not fit inside a room. We'll just keeping building the pile all summer and fall.

It is way too hot to burn in the summer. Burning is more of a winter thing to do. Summer is the time when you can see what trees are dead but in the winter it is very hard to tell if the tree is dead or not, so in the summer we cut down dead trees and then we burn in the winter.

The weather really has to be just right for burning. It cannot be too windy but it is nice just to have a little wind because when it blows on the fire it sparks it up. You want just the slightest breath and you want the grass to be wet. I have this image in my mind of the perfect time to be burning. It was a totally foggy day at Porto Bello. You could not see the water and the ground was moist. We had a huge fire and it just burned perfectly; it did not even spread from the spot. Sometimes the flame will be thirteen feet high. It is great to be out there with my dad. It is as father-son as you can possibly get.

One of my most favorite traditions is just sitting at the back of our truck with my father watching the fire and drinking a couple of beers. Sometimes my dad will tell me how to tell if people are lying. He figured it out from what he did for a living. Lying has a lot to do with facial expressions but sometimes people can pull a trick on you. Sometimes we're just quiet. We say very little but we are spending time together.

The War of Bradlee Gloves

Quinn   One of the best things about the woods is that I don't have to worry about saying something that will upset my dad. We get in arguments now that I know what I'm doing, and sometimes my dad will not like to admit that I am right, but I don't worry about it.

Working in the woods, especially burning, can be a very personal thing. If it does not go my way or my dad's way, we can actually get into arguments about it. And at the same time it brings us together because I realize that his way sometimes works better. One time my dad and I were working and we were clearing. We were about to start a burn pile and I was telling him which side to light the fire on because if you light the fire on this side, then the fire is going to go that way. And then vice versa. We got into a fight over where to light the fire and it was a huge argument. I apologized and told him I loved him and that is all that needs to be said.

We argue about where we left the tools outside and who left them there. Once he left a pair of big red clippers hanging on the tree where he'd cut it. He just left them there because he forgets.

My dad will go out wearing my boots sometimes and he'll start complaining that they're so small, saying, "These shoes suck." I'll say, "That's because they're my shoes. They're smaller than your feet."

But we probably argue the most over gloves. We have a drawer of gloves in the kitchen. Before we go out to work, my dad will rummage through it looking for a pair to wear for the day. We fight about which gloves are mine and which gloves are my dad's. Other times he'll pick the winter gloves that have fur in them to work when it is 90 degrees outside. And I'll tell him, "Those are for winter."

When he does have gloves on, we will be working and he'll take the gloves off, throw them on the ground, and leave them there. He'll keep working with his bare hands and then he'll forget where his gloves are so I'll have to go all the way back and get them for him. And then when I give them to him, he will say he doesn't need them. And he wonders why his hands are all scarred up and everything. Sometimes I will ask him where his gloves are to give him a hint but I don't think there is really a point to doing that anymore. Our family cannot keep gloves at all. It is just hopeless.

Ben   I don't think we argue. I probably tell him, "For Christ sake, don't do that," or, "Do it this way," but I try to encourage him to make his own decisions.

A few years ago, Quinn initiated quarrels with me, mostly over little things. One day while we were chopping wood, he fixated on the gloves I was wearing. He kept saying they were his gloves. I finally surrendered them and got another pair.

Quinn   I had a rare fight with my father a few years ago. I was trying to tell him something at dinner and he didn't seem able to hear me. I complained that he never seemed to be able to hear me, which made him really mad. He swore at me and left the table. Then my mother asked me why I'd hurt my father's feelings and I stormed out. I went to my room and was staring at the ceiling when my mother came in. A few minutes later I told her I didn't see any reason to live. And I meant it. I didn't have a plan but I really didn't feel like my life was worth anything. I don't remember how she reacted or the rest of the conversation. Later that night my dad came into my room and said he didn't want to go to bed feeling like this. He told me how much I meant to him and how much he loved me. I hugged him and started to cry. When he went back to bed, he told my mother that if anything happened to me he could never forgive himself.

Maybe I'm just mad at my dad for getting old. I know he's not invincible but sometimes I wish time wouldn't pass, at least when it comes to my father.

ARMCHAIR ATHLETES

Quinn   My most favorite thing to do, especially in the winter after a cold day of working out in the woods and burning, and especially if we don't burn outside, is coming in, lighting a fire in the fireplace, and just watching football, having a beer, and eating chips with my dad. I love that more than anything. I mean that is the greatest father-son bond there ever is. That is just as good as it gets.

It is one of the few moments that father and son are together and they don't have to talk if they don't want to to let each other know that they're having a good time with each other. My dad teaches me about the game of football. I'm interested in football because I love it and because my grandfather played it. But more than anything I love sitting there with my dad. When my dad was young he and his dad used to listen to Harvard football games on the radio because they didn't have TVs back then. I can only imagine how much fun that would be.

We're both Redskins fans. I guess it sort of goes with the territory. I moved to New York for a little bit when I was at the New York Film Academy and my dad said, "Whatever you do, don't become a Giants fan." Sometimes I would jokingly root against the Redskins whenever they played the Giants and I always joked that he would probably disown me if I became a Giants fan.

I come from a family of jocks. My dad played every possible sport known to man, except for fencing. He wasn't really a very good swimmer, but he played baseball, he played hockey, he played football. I think he even played basketball for a while.

Both my grandfathers were huge jocks. My mom's dad went to West Point and he was the captain of every team he played on. He was the captain of the soccer team, the fencing team, the lacrosse team, the football team, the swimming team, just everything.

My dad's dad was one of the first all-American football players. And apparently the coach absolutely loved my grandfather. While my grandfather was on the Harvard football team, they were undefeated. They beat Yale, Brown, all the biggest rivals. My grandfather was a fullback, but back then there were so few people playing football that everybody had to learn all the positions. So he was kind of a utility man. He played every position there was.

The one thing I've always wished I could do is to go back

and watch my grandfather play football. That would be absolutely amazing. He was very shy and he wasn't a huge guy, but he could apparently tackle anyone. He could bring a bull down.

I always say in my next life I am going to be an all-American football player—it would be such a great thing to be able to play college football.

But I don't carry the Bradlee jock gene. I played tennis for four years and was on the varsity team but I would end up in last place every year. I hated the competitive aspect of it. I am just not a competitive person. When you have disabilities, it's hard to compare yourself to other people. Team sports can be very competitive and the kid with VCFS will compare himself to all the other kids and then he will feel bad. So it is difficult to be on a team sport. That's why I went into solo sports like surfing and snowboarding.

There is no competition in the woods, either. I think that is one of the reasons why I love it so much and because you learn. You do nothing but learn.

LIFE CYCLE

Quinn   My dad learned everything from his dad. He doesn't ever say, "This is how I did it with my dad." But lessons learned are passed down from generation to generation. This is the way things are. This is how it is going to be. This is how it works. That is what a family tradition is and if you do not like a tradition then there are going to be some little battles going on.

I realize that I'm taking my dad's place in the woods. He still uses a chain saw but I do most of the heavy lifting now. There was a day when none of the saws would work, so he made me go get an ax. There he was at eighty-three years old, chopping wood with an ax. I finally took the ax away from him because he looked tired. He fought me a bit but not much.

Now I am reteaching him the things he taught me or am teaching new things to him. That is part of life's cycle.

Ben   Quinn is plainly stronger than I am. That became true as he grew older, and there were things he could lift that I couldn't and it became obvious that he was very much my equal in the woods, if not way ahead.

Quinn is very hardworking—he doesn't just sit around and do nothing. It's easy to get his attention. He's very industrious and he doesn't leave things undone. He'll stick to it. I'm the same. If I do it, I do it.

I've probably taught Quinn all that I can at this point. I just look forward to seeing him, having a meal with him, and working in the woods.

ALL IS EQUAL IN THE WOODS

Quinn My dad and I have a totally different relationship in the woods. He's not Ben Bradlee the great editor and I am not Quinn Bradlee the sick kid. It is a total equalizer. That is how it should be in everyday life but I feel there is a little tension. I have to do what my parents want me to do, I need to impress them just a little bit, I have to try. But in the woods I do not have to try. I will just work without even trying.

If somebody has diabetes, they are labeled differently because they have diabetes. We all have labels—rich, poor, black, white, blond, brunette. And I think "learning disabled" is a label. But when I'm with nature, I feel nature does not care about my problems. I just forget about all my problems and I can be who I want to be. I really do not have to worry about anything because I know what I am doing.

Ben I admire Quinn enormously. He's overcome obstacles that would stop a lesser man. He's fooled a lot of people into saying,

"What the hell do you mean he's learning disabled? Doesn't look learning disabled to me. Doesn't sound it, doesn't behave it." But he is. He has difficulties in comprehension. He has difficulties in reading. But he's got a lovely, joyous nature and he has a good time in life.

I'm so proud of him.

MY DAD

Quinn   My father is like a pecan tree. They grow to be two hundred years old, but they still have all their leaves and many, many branches. And they have these huge root systems and have been there forever. My dad's the same way. The branches are the stories and the different paths that my dad walked down. My dad has some of the thickest roots I've ever seen in my life. Being a genealogist, I think it comes from a thick and strong family. The roots keep my dad set in his own ways and he has a strong heart. He'll never change.

My dad was my best friend growing up. I spent all of my childhood with him. He was my mentor and my idol. He taught me the secrets to the stars and the universe out there in the woods.

I want to be like my dad because of the father that he's been to me.

A LIFE'S WORK

Sally Ben is almost eighty-nine. He is an extraordinary speci-
men. I don't know anybody his age who looks half as good or is in
better shape. But he's almost eighty-nine. Quinn is twenty-eight.
What is so touching to me is to see how their roles have subtly
and gradually reversed. Ben has taught Quinn so many things
by working with him in the woods, so many things that Quinn
would never have learned or benefited by had he led a "normal"
life. He has taught him respect for himself, for nature, and for
others. He has taught him how to love and bond. He has taught
him the importance of finishing a job once you've started and not
quitting in the middle. He has taught him hard work, patience,
and perseverance. Quinn has learned from Ben the importance
of being self-sufficient, of not complaining or being self-pitying,
of never being a victim. He has taught him the value of thinking
things through and learning from your mistakes. He has seen the
importance of being silent, of contemplation. He has learned that
everything in life doesn't happen all at once, that there are good

days and bad days, that you have to take what has been given to you, be grateful for it, and make the most of it. He has taught him courage. Most of all he has given him confidence. Ben's unwavering belief in, respect for, and love for Quinn, regardless of what was happening to him in the real world, made Quinn understand that he could accomplish anything he wanted to if he tried hard enough.

By the same token Ben has learned a lot from Quinn. Ben was always a superstar. Popular, attractive, well-to-do, intelligent, talented, and successful, Ben seemed to have it all. Except for his bout with polio, Ben has had, as he called the title of his book, "a good life." The one blip on the screen was that he had a handicapped child. That wasn't in the script. That handicap ended up dominating our lives. It was the best thing that ever happened to Ben. It humanized him. My father and Ben were World War II heroes, something Quinn never tires of hearing about when they are standing by their bonfires. Nobody would ever have called them soft. But Quinn has softened Ben. He has touched him in a way nobody else has ever been able to do.

Quinn taught his father how to love in a different way. Ben comes from an old Boston WASP family. They were rarely emotional or physically or verbally affectionate. His mother didn't even cry when he went off to war in the Pacific. (I'll never get over that.) It was very much the stiff upper lip, all the way. Quinn is one of the most physically affectionate human beings I've ever met. He must kiss and hug me and Ben five or six times a day and never finishes a conversation with either of us without saying, "I love you." (I think Ben was fifty years old before his father finally told him he loved him, though Ben never doubted it.) Because of Quinn, Ben has become a more patient, tolerant, open-minded, warm, loving, and accepting person. Quinn's book, which was published last year, is called "A Different Life." Not better, not worse, just different. In some ways he could be speaking for his father as well as for himself. Ben's life has certainly been different from what he had expected. He has Quinn to thank for that.

Quinn   I've learned so much from my parents and I never stop. But now I'm at a point in my life where I've started teaching them, too.

They ask, "When did you get so smart?"

"I am just saying what I learned from you," I tell them. "You know, I have actually listened to everything you've taught me."

POSTSCRIPT

WRITTEN ON THE OCCASION OF
QUINN'S CHRISTENING

You are truly a love child—my happiness. My joy. You are every-thing I ever wanted in my life. You fulfilled me in a way I never knew possible. I love you more than my life.

Your Mother, Sally

My first hope for you eighteen years from today would be that you are as alive and as well and as loved as you are today. If you have made it, what a lucky man I will be. You have already en-riched my life beyond—way beyond—expectations. If I didn't make it, no grief please. Remember me as you remember and value your friends, and go hard for a life that honors you, me, and them. You have already shown me, and your wonderful mother, that you can triumph and that you want to triumph. That's a big edge. Somewhere along the way I have learned to treasure this saying from the Jewish fathers: Love work, hate domination, and don't get too close to the ruling class. It's yours. And so is my love and my admiration.

Dad

ACKNOWLEDGMENTS

We would like to thank Elsa Walsh and Bob Woodward. Bob and Elsa spent many hours talking to me (Ben) and extracting all kinds of things from me that only they could do. Elsa identified the theme for the book and came up with the title, *A Life's Work*. Elsa also read the manuscript and gave invaluable advice about structure and tone. We thank them, too, for their wonderful friendship. They are a part of our family.

Jeff Himmelman, who did such a brilliant job working with me (Quinn) on my book, *A Different Life: Growing Up Learning Disabled and Other Adventures*, spent a great deal of time talking to me (Ben) about my life. Jeff also gave invaluable advice about the manuscript, immensely improving what we had written. Jeff and his wife Kirsten Lodal have become close friends in the process.

Kyle Gibson and Mitt Spears read the book and were extremely helpful in steering us toward what would be most appealing to fathers, sons, and mothers as well. Kyle is one of my (Quinn's) godmothers and we cherish them both.

Shelby Coffey, one of the greatest editors in journalism, spent many hours fine-tuning the book. It was like old times at the *Post* after I (Ben) hired him at age twenty-one. Shelby's wife Mary Lee read the manuscript as well and gave us great encouragement as a discerning reader of family literature. They have been among our dearest friends for many years.

Bob Barnett, the amazing super lawyer extraordinaire and close friend, gave us astute advice as usual.

Karen Thompson at Simon & Schuster worked tirelessly on what is always an endless process of editing and reediting the manuscript.

Our editor, the legendary Alice Mayhew, who has now overseen seven Bradlee/Quinn books, was her usual intrepid self. After more than thirty-six years of working together, Alice, too, has become a member of our family.

Alison Snyder is really responsible for this book. She was incredible at getting both of us to open up and spill our real feelings, which was quite a feat. Alison put the whole thing together and gave the book its structure. Without her we couldn't have done this.

I (Quinn) want to thank Pary for loving me.

And finally to Sally/Mom for making us keep our asses up, our noses down, and pushing forward.

Ben Bradlee and Quinn Bradlee

ABOUT THE AUTHORS

BEN BRADLEE was executive editor of *The Washington Post* from 1969 to 1991 and is currently vice president at large at the *Post*. He lives in Washington, D.C.

QUINN BRADLEE attended Landmark College, American University, and the New York Film Academy. He has made a series of short documentary films about children with learning disabilities and rare genetic syndromes, and he has launched the website FriendsofQuinn.com to create a community for LD kids and their families. He lives in Washington, D.C.